CRIMINAL JUSTICE AND SENTENCING POLICY

For my father

John Alfred Henham

Criminal Justice and Sentencing Policy

RALPH J. HENHAM
Solicitor, Reader in Law
Nottingham Trent University

Dartmouth

Aldershot • Brookfield USA • Singapore • Sydney

Published by
Dartmouth Publishing Company Limited
Gower House
Croft Road
Aldershot
Hants GU11 3HR
England

Dartmouth Publishing Company
Old Post Road
Brookfield
Vermont 05036
USA

British Library Cataloguing in Publication Data
Henham, Ralph J., 1949-
   Criminal justice and sentencing policy
   1.Sentences (Criminal procedure) - England 2.Criminal
   justice, Administration of - England
   I.Title
   344.2'05772

Library of Congress Cataloging-in-Publication Data
Library of Congress Catalog Card Number: 96-084322

ISBN 1 85521 702 3

Printed in Great Britain by the Ipswich Book Company, Suffolk

Contents

Table of Statutes

Criminal Justice Act 1988
S35
S36

Criminal Justice Act 1991
S1
S1 (2)
S1 (2) (a)
S1 (2) (b)
S1 (4)
S1 (4) (a)
S1 (4) (b)
S2 (2) (a)
S2 (2) (b)
S2 (3)
S2 (3) (a)
S2 (3) (b)
S1 (4)
S3 (1)
S3 (2)
S3 (3)
S3 (3) (a)
S3 (3) (b)
S4
S4 (1)
S4 (3) (b)
S5 (1)
S6 (1)
S18 (1)
S18 (2)
S18 (3)
S18 (5)
S25
S28
S28 (1)
S28 (2) (b)
S28 (4)

S153
Sch. 4, para. 4 (2) (d)
Sch. 8, Part II
Sch. 9, para. 10
        para. 29
        para. 30
        para. 34
        para. 40
        para. 45

Drug Trafficking Act 1994
S2 (8)
S4 (3)
S4 (4)
S4 (4) (b)
S12
S12 (5)

Drug Trafficking Offences Act 1986

Magistrates Court Act 1980
S38 (2) (b)
SS54-58

Mental Health Act 1959
Mental Health Act 1983
S1 (3)
S12
S37
S38
S41
S41 (1)
S128

Misuse of Drugs Act 1971
S5 (2)

Sch. 4, col. 5
     col. 6

Offences against the Person Act 1861
S18
S20
S27
S47

Police and Criminal Evidence Act 1984

Powers of Criminal Courts Act 1973
S2 (a)
S2 (b)
S22 (2)
S22 (3)

Sexual Offences Act 1956
S37

Theft Act 1968
S1
S9

Statutory Instruments

The Criminal Justice Act 1988 (Reviews of Sentencing)
Order 1995
The Criminal Justice and Public Order Act 1994
(Commencement No. 5) Order 1994

Table of Cases

Preface

The main purpose of this book is to examine the formation of sentencing policy with respect to certain key areas of criminal behaviour. Consequently, the main difference between this and other texts is that it provides an integrated analysis of sentencing policy formation. The discussion emphasises the development of sentencing policy through an assessment of the impact of recent legislation and sentencing guidance in the relevant key areas. Comparisons are made with other jurisdictions where appropriate and ethical and moral issues in sentencing policy development addressed. The relationship between sentencing principles, guideline judgements and Attorney-General's references is assessed in terms of its impact on sentencing policy formation. Although separate conclusions are to be drawn in respect of each key area the overall conclusion which emerges is that for sentencing policy formation to remain an integral part of criminal justice policy the respective roles of the executive, legislative and judiciary require constant clarification and direction. Suggestions are made to facilitate the attainment of this crucial objective.

Nottingham   Ralph Henham
September 1995

Acknowledgements

I would like to thank Nottingham Law School for enabling me to carry out the research on which this book is based and my family for their constant support and encouragement.

I have used, with substantial alterations and additions, some material previously published by me as follows:

Chapter 2:   "Criminal Justice and Sentencing Policy for Drug Offenders" (1994), *International Journal of the Sociology of Law*, Vol. 22, p. 223.

Chapter 3:   "Criminal Justice and the Trial and Sentencing of White Collar Offenders" (1995), *Journal of Criminal Law*, Vol. 59, Pt. 1, p. 83.

Chapter 4:   "The European Context of Sentencing Violent Offenders" (1993), *International Journal of the Sociology of Law*, Vol. 21, p. 265.

Chapter 6:   "Dangerous Trends in the Sentencing of Mentally Abnormal Offenders" (1995), *Howard Journal of Criminal Justice*, Vol. 34, No. 1, p. 10.

1 Sentencing Policy Formation

1 Introduction

It is a matter of historical fact that responsibility for the formulation of sentencing policy has devolved on the Court of Appeal (Criminal Division) as a gradually developing constitutional convention throughout the twentieth century (see Munro in Munro and Wasik (eds), 1992). As Ashworth points out, since the removal of minimum sentences in the latter part of the nineteenth century the judiciary have assumed the power to decide the appropriate sentence in individual cases and the Court of Appeal has effectively appropriated the policy-making function of Parliament in this respect (Ashworth, 1983, Ch. 2). The traditional view that it is the role of the executive to service the courts and ensure (subject to executive review) that the court's sentence is carried out has changed irrevocably. The present position represents an acknowledgement that the legislature has now *de facto* delegated a large part of its policy-making function to the judiciary. Before we consider the implications of this for contemporary sentencing policy, however, it is necessary to explain the specific significance of the Court of Appeal's sentencing principles.

2 The role of the Court of Appeal

The Court of Appeal's sentencing principles result from appeals against sentence made in the Crown Court.[1] They provide important guidance to Crown Court judges on a wide range of offences commonly dealt with by other Crown Court. Sentencing principles have developed as a consequence of the wide discretion available to sentencers which has allowed a significant degree of choice between custodial and non-custodial sentences both in terms of availability and justification. Even though this pragmatism (or eclecticism, as Walker (1985, Ch. 8, pp. 117-119) prefers to call it) has been restricted by the statutory procedures and rationale of the Criminal Justice Act 1991 there is no doubt that the Court of Appeal has largely retained its ability to use sentencing principles as an important mechanism for shaping sentencing policy in the lower courts and for providing a degree of internal consistency.

The perceived need for consistency derives from sources beyond the control of the Court of Appeal. Since retributivism is regarded as the justification in sentencing for punishment it implies that the offender is entitled to have his case determined in accordance with this principle.[2] Retributivism in sentencing therefore implies consistency. In addition, inconsistency in sentencing may also create hostility and resentment among offenders which could be counterproductive in achieving penal aims whatever these may be. Although part of the reason for this focus on disparities is concerned with penal philosophy it is also necessary to attribute some responsibility to the practical reality of sentencing. It is well-known that there is little agreement among sentencers as to what the aims of the penal system should be in terms of individual deterrence, general deterrence, reformation, rehabilitation or incapacitation. Even if it could be agreed which aims should be achieved through sentencing it would not be possible to examine their effectiveness as in the light of current research we are unable to predict accurately which penal measures are effective in preventing recidivism and which are effective deterrents. Such uncertainty is inevitably reflected by sentencers in their sentencing decisions. To add to these difficulties there is currently very little feedback to sentencers on the effectiveness of penal measures and no machinery is provided for this purpose.

Although it is implied that some kind of action should or could be taken to reduce disparities and achieve greater consistency, what sort of action is not always made clear bearing in mind that complete consistency in sentencing may be impossible to achieve. What we should perhaps be aiming for is what Hood has called "equality of consideration" (Hood, 1962, p. 14) ;

> ... by "equality" we do not mean that each case can be
> exactly compared with another, and that the decisions
> should be the same for cases "alike" in this sense. By
> "equality" we mean "equality of consideration", that is,

2

that similar general considerations can be taken into account when a decision is made.

However, such objectively desirable considerations have consistently ignored the essential subjectivism of sentence decision-making. There are numerous background variables whose interrelationship must be considered before attempting to "explain" the process whereby a judicial decision is reached. Studies by Hogarth (1971) and Hood (1972) revealed that legal (and social) constraints are perceived by sentencers in ways that are consistent with their attitudes and penal philosophies. So, although sentencers may be inconsistent with each other they remain consistent within themselves. This does not necessarily mean, however, that the penal philosophies and attitudes of sentencers are the main explanatory variables in sentencing behaviour. Indeed, my own research into the role of sentencing principles in magistrates' sentencing behaviour does not support such a generalisation (Henham, 1990, Ch. 10). It was found that adherence to the principle of individualised justice led to the conclusion that equal importance should be attached to *all* the variables revealed as relevant in sentencing studies and their interrelationship. It is not surprising, therefore, that most studies of sentencing disparity lead us to conclude that we must either tolerate disparities (although education and training may be useful in helping to reduce them) or impose uniformity.[3]

It is apparent from the foregoing discussion that the maintenance of internal consistency in sentencing policy and its jurisprudential development through sentencing principles will not deal with the fundamental subjective causes of sentencing disparity. It does, however, have the potential to make a significant contribution towards the "equality of consideration" advocated by Hood.

Notwithstanding, the Court of Appeal has been subjected to concerted criticism regarding its ability to maintain consistency through the development of sentencing principles.[4] The most serious, and so far unaddressed, issue concerns the fact that the Court of Appeal rarely has an opportunity to promulgate principles which relate to minor offences and hence the majority of those cases tried by magistrates. It has been argued that the absence of an effective prosecution right of appeal reduces the likelihood of sentences in minor cases being reviewed and it is certainly the case that the advent of the Attorney General's reference procedure under S36 Criminal Justice Act 1988 has made no material difference in this respect since it has until recently been limited to indictable offences (see Thomas, 1989 and Emmins and Scanlan, 1988, Ch. 8). The possibility exists under the amendment made to S35 Criminal Justice Act 1988 by Schedule 9, para. 34 of the Criminal Justice and Public Order Act 1994 for the Home Secretary to add cases which involve sentences of any specified description to those which the Attorney-General may refer to the Court of Appeal under the review procedure. This allows the Home Secretary to include sentences relating to specified offences triable either way and would therefore provide the potential for some guidance to be given to sentencers in magistrates' courts. However, it is probable that this potential is limited by the fact that it is only sentences at the more serious end of the penal severity scale which are likely to be reviewed[5]. Furthermore, experience of the review procedure to date confirms that it has failed to provide important guidance in cases on the borderline between custodial and non-custodial sentences (see Henham, 1994, Shute, 1994).

Wasik has also highlighted problems in the jurisprudential development of sentencing principles (Wasik, 1981). It is apparent that the Court of Appeal not only consistently fails to advert to other sentencing decisions in the course of developing sentencing principles it also tends to concentrate on the immediate case without examining the general principles behind cases of that type or their interrelationship with other types of cases. It is inevitable that this should create a lack of coherence and direction in the development of sentencing principles. These weaknesses constrain the Court of Appeal in its ability to dictate how sentencing policy should be exercised in the inferior courts. The position is compounded by the ambiguity surrounding the legal status of sentencing principles. Although not rules of law in the strict sense there is no doubt that they are intended to be binding on the lower courts[6]. It is perhaps not surprising that discretionary powers should be determined by discretionary principles but it is arguable that this is counterproductive to the maintenance of relative stability in sentencing policy[7]. The reason for this stems from the obligation to resort to judicial review if the exercise of discretionary power is to be challenged. The uncertainty and instability would be reduced and sentencing policy formation strengthened if this anomaly were to be removed.

Until recently the Court of Appeal has had a largely unfettered power to dictate how sentencing policy should be determined and exercised in the criminal courts. However, as we shall see, the changed nature of the relationship between the executive and the judiciary together with the modified structure of recent penal legislation has caused existing convention and practice to be questioned.

3   Sentencing policy and the penal crisis

The relationship between the Court of Appeal's policymaking function and the operation of the criminal justice system in its widest sense is brought sharply into focus by the continuing crisis in the British prison system. It is not our purpose here to examine the reasons behind the so-called penal crisis but its emergence during the early 1970s was concerned with the fact that recidivism statistics consistently indicated the majority of prisoners were reconvicted within two years of their release. This coincided with the announcement in 1978 of an independent inquiry by the then Home Secretary, Merlyn Rees, and the publication of the May Report in 1979[8]. The crisis in legitimacy was further exacerbated by the rapid decline in the rehabilitative ideal during the 1960s so that the then Government eventually found itself forced to re-examine the role of the short prison sentence (six months or less) as a sentencing policy initiative. Short sentences were thus justified on the basis that they were as cost effective as longer sentences since they were comparable in terms of preventing reconviction. Such negative justifications were evident in a corresponding policy initiative prompted by Lord Lane C.J. in the Court of Appeal in the *Bibi* guidelines which were similarly designed to encourage the use of shorter prison sentences in certain types of cases.[9] Lord Lane indicated that many offenders could be dealt with by sentences of six to nine months rather than eighteen months to three years' imprisonment. This was not simply desirable in the case of first offenders but also in less serious commercial burglaries, minor sexual indecency, petty frauds involving small amounts and fringe participation. Medium to longer sentences should be reserved for most robberies, serious violence, domestic burglary, planned crime for wholesale profit, and large scale drug-trafficking (although these were merely given as examples). It was stressed that what was aimed at was uniformity of approach, not sentence. Although as a major policy initiative of substantial significance the impact of *Bibi* was limited. For example, the initiative appeared to have little immediate impact apart from a slight reduction in average sentence lengths in the second half of 1980, although this was not maintained into 1981. Neither does *Bibi* appear to have had any consistent impact on the prison population. For instance, the prison population in 1980 was 42,109 (in accommodation for 38,930) but had risen to 49,578 (in accommodation for 44,179) by 1988 with a percentage occupancy rate for local prisons of 154 per cent. Further, the UK imprisonment rate has been consistently high in comparison with other EU member states (Council of Europe, 1992).

A number of additional disparate sentencing policy initiatives were also pursued during the 1980s. One principle of general applicability developed at this time was euphemistically described as the "clang of the prison gates" principle. The "clang principle" was designed to apply mainly to first offenders of previous good character on whom a short prison sentence of six months or less was expected to have a considerable deterrent impact. It was considered particularly suitable in the case of offenders convicted of theft in breach of trust and was developed as an appropriate sentencing approach in such cases.[10] Nevertheless, it is arguable that the "clang principle" was merely one aspect of a pragmatic approach to deterrent sentencing which has long been evident in Court of Appeal sentencing policy. Such sentences are often imposed not simply in the belief that they will act as effective individual deterrents but also as general deterrents since they are frequently used to deal with offences that have suddenly increased in frequency and are causing public concern.[11]

The Court of Appeal also continued to re-affirm its commitment to important policy principles which had been established for some time, such as the totality principle,[12] and the principle established in *R v Hitchcock* (1982) that a prison sentence should be the minimum necessary to achieve the purpose for which it was imposed within the constraints established by statutory provision. At that time S20 Powers of Criminal Courts Act 1973 allowed a sentencing court considerable freedom to exercise its discretionary powers by providing that it should not pass a prison sentence on someone unless of the opinion that no other method of dealing with him was appropriate. The principle in *R v Smith* (1975) also ensured that imprisonment was reserved for the gravest instances of the offence likely to occur. The significance of these constraints is difficult to assess. Ostensibly, since these constraints were designed to require the justification for imprisonment to be made explicit it can be argued that they failed to create any significant impact on the prison population which continued its inexorable rise throughout the 1980s.[13] Their collective failure to do so was taken as further evidence of the need to curtail sentencing discretion without any cogent evidence having been produced of a casual link between an incorrect sentencing approach and rising imprisonment rates.

By far the most important initiative in sentencing policy pursued by the Court of Appeal during the 1980s was a gradual refinement of the technique of delivering guideline judgements. The basic principle involves the promulgation of guidelines in specific cases which the Court of Appeal considers will provide assistance to sentencers in dealing with variance in penal severity for the same offence. Although such judgements have no greater legal force than principles established in ordinary cases[14] they have assumed immense importance in the jurisprudential development of sentencing principles although there are only some one dozen or so such judgements in existence and the issue of proportionality as between different offence categories has not been addressed.[15] Notwithstanding, guideline judgements have had a major impact on specific areas of sentencing practice (such as drug offences and social security fraud) and much of the guidance which could be of assistance to magistrates' courts is too generalised to be of much value. For example, in the drug offences guideline case of *R v Aramah* (1982) (in relation to the triable either way offence of possession of a Class B drug with intent to supply) Lord Lane C.J. stated that, in the absence of a commercial motive for the offence, it is unlikely a custodial sentence will be regarded as appropriate. Similarly, in relation to cases of simple possession of a Class B drug *Aramah* simply states that a fine will usually be appropriate. In neither case is there a detailed appraisal of the correct sentencing approach in such cases by reference to specific aggravating or mitigating factors and their relative significance. This kind of practical refinement became evident in the Magistrates' Association's Sentencing Guidelines[16] following the enactment of the Criminal Justice Act 1991.

Similar criticisms may be directed against another major sentencing policy initiative instigated by S36 Criminal Justice Act 1988 - the Attorney General's reference procedure - which effectively permits the prosecution to appeal against unduly lenient sentences (see Henham, 1994, Shute, 1994). The reference procedure provides the Court of Appeal with the potential to deliver useful and consistent sentencing guidance yet it has been restricted in its ability to provide a mechanism for shaping sentencing policy by the limited number of cases referable to it. The Court of Appeal's power to develop the reference procedure constructively is further restricted by the approach to reference cases suggested by Lord Lane C.J. in *Attorney General's Reference (No. 4 of 1989)* (1990). This approach requires that the Court of Appeal should only consider a sentence as being unduly lenient where it falls outside the range of sentences which the judge, applying his mind to all the relevant factors, could reasonably consider appropriate. The relevant factors and their reasonableness are derived from and constrained by the relevant range of sentences currently determined by the Court of Appeal, regard being had to reported cases and, more particularly, guidance given by the Court in guideline cases. The approach therefore interprets the concept of undue leniency in a particularly restrictive fashion. In *Attorney General's Reference (No. 5 of 1989) (Hill-Trevor)* (1989) Lord Lane C.J.

had re-iterated that the issue at stake in reference cases was that public confidence in the judicial system would be damaged if the sentence were to remain as it had been passed. However, the Court decided this case without considering exactly what the test of public confidence actually demanded. It was simply assumed that public confidence could be equated with the need to ensure that judicial errors of principle did not occur. This is a particularly narrow interpretation of the public perception of justice since it interprets the public desire for justice as being capable of fulfilment through the application of existing sentencing principles and guidance. It therefore fails to respond to public demands since it is essentially backward-looking and concerned with legal form. This in turn hinders the constructive development of sentencing guidance which becomes reactive rather than innovative and responsive to perceptions of public need. A clear example of the failure of the reference procedure to accord with public perceptions and fulfil its public relations potential is provided by *R v Bray* (1994) where the five year prison sentence imposed by Drake J. at Plymouth Crown Court of a shoplifter convicted of the manslaughter of a schoolboy was not referred to the Court of Appeal by the Attorney-General. The sentence attracted considerable media criticism as being unduly lenient.[17] In the course of his judgement Drake J. had told the court that although he would have liked to have passed a longer sentence he had been prevented from doing so by Court of Appeal guidelines which indicated that a two to five year prison sentence was appropriate in such cases. Although the reasoning of both the Crown Court judge and the Attorney-General was unimpeachable from a jurisprudential standpoint the logic of the sentence clearly failed to satisfy the public perception of justice. The sentence of 180 hours community service given to former financial adviser Roger Levitt at Southwark Crown Court in November 1993 when his investment group had collapsed with debts of £34 million understandably received almost universal condemnation.[18] However, since Levitt had pleaded guilty to an either way offence it was not possible for the Attorney-General to refer the sentence to the Court of Appeal as unduly lenient.[19] Notwithstanding the extension of referable cases in March 1994, it did not include the majority of dishonesty offences, burglary and drug offences. The potential now exists to remedy these deficiencies since Schedule 9, para. 34, Criminal Justice and Public Order Act 1994 amended S35 Criminal Justice Act 1988 by enabling the Home Secretary to add cases involving sentences of any specified description to those which the Attorney-General may refer to the Court of Appeal under the existing procedure.

The Court of Appeal's sentencing guidance and the Attorney-General's reference procedure were both given a prominent role in the sentencing reforms which resulted in the Criminal Justice Act 1991. This was made clear by the Government White Paper published in 1990 (para. 2.20);

> The new legislative provisions, the maximum penalties for each offence, the guidance from the Court of Appeal and the Attorney-General's new power to refer over-lenient sentences for very serious offenders to the Court of Appeal, should all contribute to the development of coherent sentencing practice which can be disseminated to the court by the Judicial Studies Board.[20]

It is immensely significant that the then Government effectively entrusted the future success of its sentencing reforms to the judiciary (in the form of the Court of Appeal) but the failure to clarify their status or the nature of their role created both tension and uncertainty once the reforms had been implemented. The reason for this was concerned with the fact that the reforms themselves represented a fundamental change in the philosophical justification for punishment to a sentencing policy based on just deserts.[21]

The 1991 legislation itself was designed to provide a new and more coherent framework for sentencing whilst at the same time rejecting the idea of strict legislative control. This ambiguous position meant that executive control of sentencing policy was re-asserted at the same time as the judiciary were being required to implement the details of the policy in question. Although the executive has always retained responsibility for the overall formulation of sentencing policy the 1991 reforms actually reduced the scope for judicial discretion to such an extent that its ability to dictate sentencing policy for specific offence categories was severely restricted.[22] Hence, the Court of Appeal found itself facing the need to implement a policy which reduced its overall policy-making role formerly exemplified by such initiatives as the *Bibi* guidelines.

4 The impact of recent legislation

There is no doubt that the Criminal Justice Act 1991 marked a significant watershed in the philosophy and practice of sentencing. In terms of sentencing policy formation the Act heralded a major restriction in judicial practice through the replacement of tariff sentencing principles[23] with the imposed system contained in the 1991 Act introduced by the seriousness criterion in S1 (2) (a). The tariff sentencing system had drawn a clear distinction between tariff and individualised sentences each of which was designed to reflect different penal aims. The choice between a tariff sentence and an individualised sentence was described by Thomas (1979) as the primary decision. It is important to record the fact that the initial sentencing approach was dictated by judicial discretion rather than legislative imperative. The tariff sentence was essentially a sentence designed to reflect the offender's culpability, a process which involved reflecting offence gravity against the pattern of sentences for offences of that kind and subsequently making allowances for mitigating factors which might reduce the offender's culpability. Where the sentencer's aim was to influence the offender's future behaviour the primary decision would result in an individualised sentence based on an assessment of the probable future behaviour of the offender and his likely response to a particular penal measure ranging from supervision, treatment or preventative confinement. The individualised measure was generally favoured where there was no obvious need for a tariff sentence in circumstances indicating the likelihood that the offender would respond. For this reason it was considered particularly appropriate in the case of young offenders, psychiatric cases, intermediate and persistent recidivists. The statutory criteria imposed by the 1991 Act failed to elucidate the detailed requirements relating to seriousness and how they could be achieved within particular offence categories. The Act also failed to indicate how proportionality was to be maintained as between different offence categories. This absence of statutory guidance was compounded by the fact that the same criteria were applied to both custodial and non-custodial sentences. The success of Government policy initiatives to promote community sentences as realistic punishments in the community and the success of the ill-fated unit fine scheme was entrusted to the interpretative guidance of the Court of Appeal. However, nothing was done to address the general lack of guidance relating to non-custodial sentences evident in Court of Appeal sentencing principles.

The early release provisions contained in Part II of the 1991 Act[24] also made it imperative for the Lord Chief Justice, Lord Taylor, to deliver a Practice Statement on the Criminal Justice Act 1991 which coincided with the implementation of the main provisions of the Act in October 1992 as follows:

It is therefore vital for all sentencers in the Crown Court to realise that sentences on the "old scale" would under the "new" Act result in many prisoners actually serving longer in custody than hitherto. It has been an axiomatic principle of sentencing policy until now that the Court should decide the appropriate sentence in each case without reference to questions of remission or parole... we have decided that a new approach is essential... it will be necessary when passing a custodial sentence in the Crown Court to have regard to the actual period likely to be served and, as far as practicable, to the risk of offenders serving substantially longer under the new system than would have been normal under the old. Existing guideline judgements should be applied with these considerations in mind... having taken the above considerations into account sentencers must, of course, exercise their individual judgement as to the appropriate sentence to be passed and nothing in this statement is intended to restrict that independence.

It was predicted by Thomas (1992, p. 12) that unless prisoners serving medium term sentences (from about 12 months to about three years) had their sentences discounted by roughly one-third under the new system it would result in a general lengthening of prison terms served by inmates in this category. Such prisoners had the best chance of release on licence under the old system. Notwithstanding, its obvious significance there remain two important unanswered questions relating to the implementation of the Practice Statement which are crucial to its assessment as a major contribution to sentencing policy and practice:

1.   Did the Statement have any consistent effect on sentencing practice?

2.   Did the Statement change the judicial *approach* to sentence decision-making?

Judicial interpretation of the 1991 Act's provisions has concentrated on the development of sentencing principles which seek to interpret and elucidate the relevant criteria in relation to each offence type and there does not appear to have been a concerted policy to embrace the just deserts principles embodied in the Act. There has, nevertheless, been evidence of a desire to re-assert elements of pre-Act sentencing policy and so

11

correspondingly judicial discretion and pragmatic sentencing practice. Such an approach was evident in *R v Cunningham* (1993) where the Court of Appeal indicated that the prevalence of an offence was a legitimate factor to be considered by a sentencer in determining not only the length of a custodial sentence but also whether it crossed the custody threshold in the first place.[25] The significance of this pronouncement also lay in the fact that the Court did not feel constrained by the rationale of the 1990 White Paper which had made explicit the principle that deterrence could affect the length of a custodial sentence provided the sentence was commensurate with the seriousness of the offence or offences for which it was passed.[26] An extension of this judicial encroachment on policy-making was seen in *R v Kempley* (1994) where Russell L.J. in the Court of Appeal stated that there *had* to be a deterrent element in any sentence imposed on someone found in possession of the Class A drug ecstasy with intent to supply. A sentence of five years' imprisonment on a first offender was consequently imposed. Adherence to notions of judicial flexibility and discretion were similarly evident in *Cunningham* from the Court of Appeal's assertion that the 1992 Practice Statement did not require sentencers to reduce sentence lengths in accordance with a fixed scale since a discretionary element should remain in the case of longer sentences. It was important to maintain a pragmatic approach in deciding on the appropriateness of the sentence within the parameters established by the 1991 Act. The Court of Appeal had initially sought to assist itself and others in this task by adopting the so-called "right-thinking member of the public" test (relating to S1 (4) Criminal Justice Act 1982 and developed by Lawton L.J. in *R v Bradbourn* (1985)), in *R v Cox* (1993) and *R v Baverstock* (1993). Ashworth (1994, pp. 154, 155) opined that the Court of Appeal has failed to develop this test constructively and that it is, in any event, counterproductive since it is too vague to be connected to recognised sentencing principles. To reduce the level of custodial sentences for less serious offences and provide more useful guidance for lower courts he advocates that a judicial principle or presumption should be adopted whereby pure property offences below a certain value should not result in a custodial sentence. This would, of course, give full expression to the policy-making role reserved to the Court of Appeal by the 1990 White Paper and the 1991 Act. It would also provide a judicial principle whose effect on the prison population would be relatively easy to ascertain. However desirable the suggestion it is unlikely that the Court of Appeal would ever go as far as re-defining its sentencing jurisdiction in this way into what amounts to clear executive territory. The ineffectiveness of present Government criminal justice policy, evident from recent prison statistics suggesting a continued rise in the prison population.[27] cannot be attributed to the Court of Appeal policy pronouncements on sentencing with any degree of confidence. It may be the case that Government equivocation in sentencing approach and policy has had little impact on Court of Appeal sentencing policy or, alternatively, that deliberate strategic changes in sentencing policy instigated by the Court of Appeal (if any) have had a negligible impact on the prison population in any event. It is difficult to measure firstly, what effect suggested changes in sentencing approach actually have on the exercise of judicial discretion and, secondly, whether such correlations (if any) can then be seen between the exercise of such judicial discretion and trends in the prison population.

However, Government initiatives in sentencing policy soon evaporated into a series of legislative changes which appeared to be informed by the dictates of political expediency rather than coherent long term strategic considerations.[28] The Criminal Justice Act 1993 provided evidence of a re-alignment of sentencing policy towards punishments and deterrence at the expense of proportionality and just deserts. Most significantly, S1 of the 1991 Act was amended by S66 (1) of the 1993 Act to permit the court to consider not only the present offence but also *all* associated offences when considering whether to impose a custodial sentence on the grounds of its seriousness. This permitted the sentencing court to aggregate a series of minor offences in deciding whether the custody threshold had been breached. Corresponding amendments were made by S66 (2) to allow the court to consider all associated offences when determining the length of a custodial sentence (see Brownlee, 1994). These legislative changes were significant in policy terms since they appeared to indicate a deliberate move away from the 1991 Act agenda of diverting small-scale recidivist offenders from custodial to community-based sentencing alternatives by promoting community sentences as punishment in the community. The amendment of S3 (3) (a) of the 1991 Act by S66 (3) of the 1993 Act further re-inforced this interpretation of events by requiring the court to take into account all such information as is available to it about the *offence* and any associated offences combined with it. Thomas (1993a) suggested that S3 (3) impliedly prevented courts from considering offender, as opposed to offence, information when assessing seriousness under S1. This eliminates causal issues from the seriousness criterion. In effect, therefore, offender information is only able to influence decisions relating to offence seriousness through personal mitigation under S28 (1) of the 1991 Act. This important principle was established by *R v Cox* (1993) in which the Court of Appeal stated that S28 (1) is relevant at the stage when the

13

court is deciding whether to impose a custodial sentence *ab initio* (S1 (2) (a)) and not simply on the question of length (S2 (2) (a)).

The amendment of S29 of the 1991 Act by S66 (6) of the 1993 Act was a further aspect of the re-alignment of Government sentencing policy towards punishment and deterrence rather than just deserts. This was achieved by the amended S29 removing the restriction that the courts were only allowed to take account of the offence and one other associated offence in considering whether to impose a custodial or community sentence on seriousness grounds. The amended S29 (1) instead provided that when considering the seriousness of the current offence or offences previous convictions and failure to respond to previous sentences may be taken into account. The broad nature of the re-drafted S29 (1) appears to give the sentencer complete discretion as to what stage an offender's previous convictions are taken into account, particularly when taken in conjunction with S28. For example, Ashworth and Gibson (1994) have recently suggested that the amended wording of S29 (1) may have the effect of allowing previous convictions and sentences to lift a particular offence over the custody threshold (ibid. p. 106);

> "Thus, the notion of proportionality to the seriousness of the current offence, so pivotal to the scheme of the 1991 Act, has been weakened. Prisons and young offender institutions may once again fill with people who have been sentenced on their record rather than for a serious offence."

Wasik and von Hirsch (1994), however, consider that the reference to "failure to respond" in the new S29 (1) should be construed narrowly as only relevant in considering the seriousness of the offence. They argue that an offender's failure to respond is relevant only in so far as it impinges on his culpability as construed by the seriousness criterion embodied in the 1991 Act. Hence, the current offence still continues to determine the "seriousness" threshold or ceiling beyond which the sentencer cannot proceed. Wasik and von Hirsch also suggest (ibid. p. 415) that the new S29 (1) provides clearer statutory authority than its predecessor for the doctrine of progressive loss of mitigation.[29] This debate again provides an illustration of how the nature and extent of sentencing provisions may be determined by the Court of Appeal not simply in their technical interpretation but, crucially, in the context of its policy-making function.

14

Section 66 (6) of the 1993 Act amended S29 (2) of the 1991 Act to provide that the fact an offence has been committed on bail should be regarded as an aggravating factor in considering the seriousness of the present offence. Previously, in *R v Baverstock* (1993), the Court of Appeal held that the sentencing court had a discretion in such cases. By introducing a mandatory requirement it was suggested the provision may have an adverse effect on the prison population (see Ashworth and Gibson, 1994, p. 109) given the large number of offences committed by offenders whilst on bail.

Finally, the 1993 Criminal Justice Act saw perhaps the greatest *volte face* in recent penal history with the wholesale abolition of the unit fine system introduced in the 1991 Act by S65 and Schedule 30. This effectively initiated a return to the previous system and simultaneously made the prospect of increased fine default and subsequent imprisonment more immediate for unemployed and poor offenders (Ashworth and Gibson, 1994, pp. 106-108).

There are cogent grounds for suggesting that certain 1991 Act provisions indicated a distinct policy shift from protectionism to welfarism. For example, new criteria for imposing custody on an offender who is or appears to be mentally disordered were imposed by S4 (discussed in Chapter 7). In addition to requiring a medical report in all cases where an offender is, or appears to be, mentally disordered unless the court deems it unnecessary, the court must also consider the likely effect of a custodial sentence on any mental condition and treatment that may be available. This appears to represent a distinct improvement on the pre-Act position where it was assumed that the prison authorities would simply remove mentally disordered offenders to secure hospital accommodation, if necessary. Nevertheless, such treatment provisions have been effectively subsumed to the wider imperative of punishment through just deserts (see Chapter 7). This has produced an environment where the due process rights of certain offenders, such as mentally abnormal offenders, are compromised or threatened. More specifically, it may be argued that the protectionist provisions contained in SS1 (2) (b) and 2 (2) (b) of the 1991 Act constitute such a threat to mentally abnormal offenders since they are more likely to commit "violent" or "sexual" harm within the meaning of the Act and consequently be adjudged dangerous. As we shall see, similar arguments may be put forward in connection with the sentencing of drug offenders (see Chapter 3). It may also be argued that the strict probation breach and treatment conditions contained in the 1991 Act coupled with the more restrictive changes instigated by the 1993 Act have effectively reduced the

15

range of sentencing options strategically available to addicted drug offenders.

The immediate impact of the 1991 Criminal Justice Act on the prison population was a fall in the proportionate use of immediate custody for indictable offences particularly among offenders with a substantial number of previous convictions (Home Office, 1993a). However, for male offenders with five or less previous convictions aged 21 and over the proportionate use of immediate custody actually increased by approximately two per cent in all courts over the relevant period. The proportionate use of fines and community sentences also increased over the relevant period. It may be convincingly argued that the 1993 Criminal Justice Act is unlikely to sustain this positive trend since the Home Office's own projected figures, based on pre-1991 Act sentencing policy, gives the total prison population in 2001 as 51,600 compared with 45,800 in 1992. These figures take into account the slower projected growth element of the 1991 Act but not the 1993 Act effect which is likely to reverse the effect of the former (Home Office, 1993b).

Although the most recent legislative change, the Criminal Justice and Public Order Act 1994, contains a number of provisions which will have a far-reaching effect on the operation of the entire criminal justice system the two most significant changes in terms of sentencing policy formation concern reviews of sentencing and sentencing discounts. The amendment to S35 Criminal Justice Act 1988 by Schedule 9, para. 34 of the 1994 Act enables the Home Secretary to add cases of any specified description to those which the Attorney-General may refer to the Court of Appeal for a review of the sentence (see earlier discussion). Section 48 of the 1994 Act provides that, when sentencing an offender who has pleaded guilty, a court shall take into account the stage in the proceedings at which he indicated the intention to do so and the circumstances in which the indication was given. If as a result the court imposes a punishment less severe than it would otherwise have done it must state in open court that it has done so. The announcement by the Home Secretary to introduce a statutory system of sentence discounts for guilty pleas in February 1994[32] followed the recommendation of the Royal Commission on Criminal Justice (1993) which had proposed a process described as a "sentencing canvass" whereby the defence would instigate a procedure permitting the judge to indicate the maximum sentence discount were the defendant to plead guilty. There were strong policy reasons for adopting such a procedure since the so-called "cracked trials" problem had reached serious proportions with some 83 per cent of those defendants electing Crown Court trial changing their plea to guilty. The Royal Commission therefore recommended (1993, Ch. 7, para. 56) that discussions on the level of charge should take place as early as possible to reduce the need for cases to be listed as contested trials. Although the Royal Commission had also recommended that a sentence discount policy should be kept under review in order to monitor its impact on ethnic minorities S48 contains no procedural safeguards in this respect. This is a serious omission in the light of Hood's (1992) research indicating that more black (i.e. Afro-Caribbean) than white defendants plead not guilty in Crown Court trials which results in lengthier custodial sentences due to existing sentence discounts given in exchange for guilty pleas. Thomas (1994a) has also indicated the presence of a number of procedural anomalies in the new provisions. For example, firstly, whether there is an obligation to allow a discount in all cases where a guilty plea is entered or merely an early plea and, secondly, the nature of the relationship between the protective provisions in S2 (2) (b) of the 1991 Act which are mandatory and the obligation to consider sentence discounts contained in S48 of the 1994 Act. The main policy implication of sentence discounts is that of undermining the presumption of innocence by relieving the prosecution of the legal and moral obligation to prove its case. The new section fails to recognise that the strength of the prosecution case will be a relevant determinant of the extent of any discount, or, if pleas to lesser charges within the indictment fall within the scope of the procedure. As described in Chapter 4 such factors have proved of considerable significance in fraud cases. It is also arguable that statutory sentence discounts can lead to an increase in "real" offence sentencing and produce a system which discourages potential contested trials by penalising those who plead not-guilty (Tonry and Coffee, 1992). Ultimately, it leads to an increase in prosecutorial discretion. The Court of Appeal's response to what appears to be a policy of political and administrative expediency will be crucial to its success. Although the principle of providing an appropriate discount for a guilty plea is well established (see Thomas, 1970, p. 195)[33] the Court of Appeal has exhibited a marked reluctance to specify the extent of such discounts. A continued failure in this respect will restrict the utility of any sentencing guidance since it is otherwise impossible to discern what the "correct" sentence should actually be.

5   Conclusions and reform

Sentencing policy formulation has recently been at the centre of an increasing rift between the executive and the judiciary over the future

17

direction and purpose of the criminal justice system. There have been a large number of public disagreements regarding important aspects of recent Government penal policy. The most notable examples concern the attack on due process rights such as the right to silence contained in the Criminal Justice and Public Order Bill 1993[34], the abolition of which had been rejected by the majority of the Royal Commission on Criminal Justice 1993 (Ch. 4, paras. 22-3). Considerable concern was also expressed by Lord Taylor C.J. in connection with the introduction of revised sentencing guidelines for magistrates issued by the Magistrates' Association in September 1993.[35] The main criticism was directed at the introduction of "entry points" for each offence which, it was felt, would result in the raising of the tariff for certain offences and consequently contribute to an increase in the prison population. Finally, proposals to introduce sentence discounts and relax the requirements for mandatory pre-sentence reports contained in the Criminal Justice and Public Order Bill 1993 similarly provoked judicial comment. More general criticism of Government penal strategy was delivered in a scathing attack by Woolf L.J. in October 1993[36] on proposed changes to the criminal justice system whilst Lord Taylor C.J. and two former Home Secretaries were vociferous in their condemnation of what was perceived as increased political interference in the control of police forces contained in the Police and Magistrates' Courts Bill 1993.[37]

The problems of increased political constraint and interference in the operation of the criminal justice system and the attempts to fetter and direct judicial discretion through statutory means pose a potential constitutional dilemma. It is arguable that this politicisation of sentencing policy formation can only be resisted by a re-assertion of judicial control and independence in trial and sentencing issues. The classical notion of the social contract which exists between citizens and criminal justice agencies is relevant in this context since it must surely be regarded as a central tenet of the administration of justice that certain guarantees should exist regarding the inviolability of citizens rights from abrogation by state institutions. These rights should require that a balance be achieved between maintaining the presumption of innocence through due process and, on the other hand, justifying punishment in its nature and extent. The classical objection to judicial discretion must be waived as a condition of the re-assertion of basic rights which have been eroded by executive action (see Radzinowicz, 1966, Ch. 1). It is axiomatic that these rights can only be protected by asserting the independence of agents of social control within the criminal justice system. Although greater autonomy can only achieve public acceptability through increased training and revision of judicial selection procedures it is arguable that a more stringent control mechanism in the form of increasingly rigid sentencing guidelines is required in exchange for a public re-assertion of the principle of judicial independence in sentencing policy formation.

In essence, the present position can perhaps be summarised most effectively in the following propositions:

(i) Judicial discretion is by definition *restrictable* as opposed to controllable. Research by Hogarth (1971) and Hood (1972) would suggest that legal and social constraints are perceived in ways that minimise inconsistencies with sentencers' existing attitudes and beliefs.

(ii) If judicial discretion is only restrictable then executive or legislative attempts to manipulate sentencing policy through changing the judicial *approach* to custodial sentencing are doomed to failure where the judiciary is relied upon as the major plank for implementing such reforms.

(iii) Government penal policy attacks on basic due process rights have provoked a situation where the concept of judicial independence needs to be re-asserted. Some commentators have even argued that a Bill of Rights is necessary.[38]

These issues are further explored in Chapter 8.

References

1. Apart from a few minor exceptions, the Court of Appeal (Criminal Division) can hear appeals relating to all cases triable in the Crown Court.
2. See *R v Reeves* (1964).
3. See, for example, Gaudet (1933), Mannheim, Spencer and Lynch (1957), Shoham (1959), Green (1961), Nagel (1962), Smith and Blumberg (1967), Wheeler (1968), Hogarth (1971), Hood (1972), Tarling (1979), Moxon (1988).

4.   See, for example, Wasik (1981).

5.   The Criminal Justice Act 1988 (Reviews of Sentencing) Order 1995 which came into effect on 8 February 1995 extended the range of cases in respect of which the power was exercisable to include fraud cases triable in the Crown Court under the notice of transfer procedure established by Part 1, Criminal Justice Act 1987, (see Chapter 3).

6.   Court of Appeal sentencing decisions have been treated as rules of substantive law for the purposes of the precedent system and the full court has overruled previous decisions in the interests of justice when dealing with a discretionary principle rather than a substantive legal rule;   see *R v Jackson* (1973).   A sentencing principle may not, however, be certified as involving a question of law of general public importance for the purpose of an appeal to the House of Lords; *R v Ashdown* (1973).   Thomas has argued that sentencing principles should be treated as equivalent to substantive legal rules for the purpose of the precedent system (Thomas, 1979, p. 4) and has commented adversely on the current anomalous situation, see Thomas, 1982, p. 383 and 1983, p. 491.

7.   In *R v Johnson* (1994) the Court of Appeal emphasised that when sentencing a judge must "pay attention to the guidance given by the Court of Appeal and sentences should be broadly in line with guideline cases, unless there were factors applicable to the particular case which require or enable the judge to depart from the normal level of sentence.   In such special cases the judge should indicate clearly the factor or factors which in his judgement allow departure from the tariff set by this Court.   What a judge must not do is to state that he is applying some personal tariff because he considers the accepted range of sentences to be too high or too low" *per* Roch L.J.   Although this approach is frequently identifiable, see for example *Attorney-General's Reference No. 20 of 1994 (R v Maclennan)* (1995), the Court of Appeal occasionally displays a scant disregard for its own previous decisions and eschews any principled approach.   As Thomas states in his commentary on *R v Townsend* (1995) (Thomas, 1995, p. 182).

> If the Court of Appeal does not take its own previous decisions seriously, it is unlikely that sentencers in other courts will do so;   there is a risk that the Court will undermine its own

authority, and any hope of achieving a consistent approach to sentencing in the Crown Court will be lost.

See also Thomas (1994b).

8. For detailed analysis of the origins and constituent elements of the crisis, see Fitzgerald and Sim (1979).

9. See *R v Bibi* (1980).

10. See *R v Upton* (1980) and *R v Smedley* (1981).

11. See for example, *R v Storey* (1973), *R v Hall and Brown* (1980) (mugging), *R v Ford and Ors* (1981) (smuggling of cocaine), *R v Whitton* (1986) (soccer hooliganism), *R v Dythe and Redford* (1987) (pickpocketing).

12. See, for example, *R v Dillon* (1983).

13. It is important to note that these restrictions on custodial sentencing existed long before the Criminal Justice Act 1991. If this argument is correct there was no reason to suppose that legislative restrictions would be any more effective.

14. The extent to which they should encourage a consistent and principled approach was considered recently in *R v Johnson* (1994).

15. The following examples have had a major impact on sentencing practice; *R v Aramah* (1982) (drugs), *R v Barrick* (1985) (theft in breach of trust), *R v Billam* (1986) (rape), *R v Stewart* (1987) (social security fraud).

16. The first sentencing guidelines adopting this approach were issued by the Magistrates' Association in 1992. For initial analysis see Wasik and Turner, 1993. More controversial guidelines recommending specific "entry points" were issued in September 1993. It is often overlooked that these guidelines are not binding on magistrates' courts and may be adopted, modified or substituted in order to suit local conditions.

17. See, for example, *The Times,* 17 March 1994, 14 April 1994 and 27 June 1994.

18. See, for example, *The Times,* 27 and 30 November 1993.

19. The Criminal Justice Act 1988 (Reviews of Sentencing) Order 1995 which came into effect on 8 February 1995 extended the range of cases in respect of which the Attorney-General's reference procedure may be exercised to include fraud cases tried in the Crown Court following the notice of transfer procedure established by Part 1, Criminal Justice Act 1987. Note, however, that Levitt

had pleaded guilty to the either way offence of misleading FIMBRA having pleaded not guilty to two charges of fraudulent trading.

20. Wasik and von Hirsch (1990) made the following important criticisms of the just deserts sentencing policy proposed in the 1990 White Paper:-

1) Basic articulation of proportionality was not discussed in the White Paper. This should consist of a basic norm that sanctions should be in just proportion to the gravity of offences. A standard definition of crime seriousness should be provided i.e. it should be determined by:

   a) the harmfulness (see Ashworth (1995)) (or potential harmfulness) of the criminal conduct, and,

   b) the culpability of the actor

2) the weight to be given to prior offending should be clarified. A "progressive loss of mitigation" test was suggested.

3) Aggravation and mitigation had to be examined in a way consistent with the proportionality rationale. Therefore, these factors must relate to the harm or culpability of the conduct. They should include:-

   a) particular *cruelty* in the commission of the crime

   b) vulnerability of the victim

   c) provocation by the victim

   d) peripheral involvement on the actor's part

   e) diminished capacity or understanding on the actor's part

   f) extraordinary hardship to the defendant

4) Desert requirements were compromised by the proposal to allow predictive confinement by sentencers for persistent violent and sexual offenders. Additional increases in penalty levels could not be justified on desert grounds as offenders were already severely dealt with under the existing "dualtrack" system. Because of known inaccuracy of predictive techniques additional punishment on ground of anticipated dangerousness was flawed.

5) On community penalties the so-called "cafeteria" approach was dangerous as it ran counter to the Government's expressed preference for penalty scaling and

standardisation of breach arrangements. The best way foreward was for sentencers in each case to select a "head" community sanction appropriate to the offence, only adding other elements for good reason and where additional elements did not make the overall sanction disproportionate to the seriousness of the offence committed.

6)   The White Paper offered no proposals on the subject of breach which implied that if prison was invoked to punish such breaches more people would end up being confined than before. Also, breach hardly seemed comparable to a serious offence.

7)   Injection of greater proportionality into the parole machinery raised the issue of the relationship between sentencing and parole decisions. Traditionally, sentencers had been forbidden to take account of the likely effects of remission and parole release arrangements on the individual sentences they passed; *Maguire* (1957) (remission), *Kenway and Cunningham* (1985) (parole). The Carlisle Committee had suggested that any new changes should be taken into account by sentencers thereby shortening sentences across the board. The Government had not dealt with this issue so it was likely sentencers would continue to regard release arrangements as irrelevant to sentencing. Wasik and von Hirsch suggested that some clear indication of the scale of reduction was required by either;

    a)   Practice Direction
    b)   Statutory Directive
Suggestion a) was achieved in 1992.

21.   Galligan (1981) had earlier carefully summarised the sentencing policy implications of a just deserts approach:-

1)   The sentencing decision was concerned only with assessing offenders deserts according to the seriousness of the offence and did not concern itself with forward-looking goals.

2)   The sentencer had no discretion to choose among different and possibly conflicting goals - he only needed to make an assessment of offenders' comparative as opposed to natural deserts. Consequently, it was not so much that one penalty was uniquely deserved but that it was deserved when comparison was made with the way others have been treated i.e. proportionality.

3)   There was no room for indeterminacy in sentences as the whole point of sentencing was to assess as precisely as possible the deserved sentence. The need for parole was therefore largely removed.

Galligan saw the main criticisms of just deserts in sentencing decisions as concerned with: The assessment of seriousness (i.e. the degree of wrongdoing and culpability of the defendant) which was difficult to assess. Wrongdoing involves questions about harm - is it harm caused, risked or intended? - whilst "culpability" involved an analysis of intention, motives, purposes, pressures and influences

Galligan suggested the following problems were faced by reformers:-

a)
    i)   whether to allow judges wide discretion to decide seriousness and therefore the deserts. This may lead to uncontrollable subjective assessments or,

    ii)   whether to stipulate factors that would count towards seriousness and limit judges to them. This would risk assessments becoming crude and approximate.

b)   What would count towards seriousness?
    Deserts was backward looking. For example did past convictions add to a man's deserts or did they suggest the need for a stiffer deterrent? It was not certain which so utilitarian advantages such as deterrence, rehabilitation and social protection could yet be obtained in the name of desert.

c)   Was a deserts sentencing system desirable?
    i)   There was a danger that if severe protective penalties were passed on offenders classified as dangerous it would keep the range of penalties in the system high to maintain consistency.

    ii)   It would have the effect of levelling-up at the bottom of the penalty range.

    iii)   It would lead to the abandonment of measures which were humanitarian and reformative in spirit.

Ashworth (1989) has detailed some of the advantages of "Just Deserts" as follows:-

24

1) Coherence in the sentencing system - it would avoid the "cafeteria" approach. However, this could equally apply to deterrence.

2) Consistent and principled sentencing - although the ideal solution was to structure sentencing discretion according to stated standards thereby ensuring discretion was exercised according to legal principle while retaining judicial flexibility for cases where combinations of facts did not fall within the guidelines.

3) Public acceptability and comprehensibility - according to Walker and Hough (1988) the most popular aim (44 per cent) was to "give the offender what he deserved" although there was ignorance about the effects of parole on prison sentences. Deserts emphasis on "real time" was considered important.

22. Within those categories the Court of Appeal retained considerable autonomy to interpret and develop the "seriousness" criterion.

23. See Thomas, 1979, Ch. 1 and also Thomas, 1967, p. 503.

24. The procedures confined parole to those sentenced to four years or more imprisonment. Where sentenced to less than four years, the Secretary of State may release on licence at the half-way stage, but, if between such release and the end of the period covered by the original sentence, the offender commits an imprisonable offence he may be recalled to serve the balance of the original sentence outstanding at the time of the fresh offence. Where sentenced to a four year or more determinate sentence prisoners are released on licence after serving two-thirds of the sentence and become eligible for parole at the half-way stage. Prisoners remain at risk following release in the same way as short term prisoners.

25. The court made it clear that the seriousness of an offence was affected by how many people it harmed and to what extent. In such circumstances, the sentence commensurate with the seriousness of the offence might need to be higher than elsewhere. Thomas, 1993b, p. 151 opined that the court was referring to consideration of the custody threshold in S1 (2) (a) as well as to length of sentence under S2 (2) (a).

26. Hence, general deterrence would not allow a sentencer to pass a custodial sentence longer than justified by the seriousness of the offence although prevalence could justify a longer sentence by

making the offence itself more serious. In this way the court effectively restricted the availability of exemplary sentences.

27. If those figures prove correct they will mark an increase of 7,900 in the prison population since 1982, a percentage increase of 18 per cent (see Home Office 1993a, 1993b).

28. The proposals which formed the basis of the Criminal Justice Bill 1993 were announced in November 1993 following the Home Secretary's tough law and order speech at the Conservative Party Conference in 1993. For evaluation of the increased politicisation of criminal justice see Lacey, 1994.

29. This principle asserts that proportionality must be maintained between the punishment and the gravity of the offence. In the context of modern desert theory it should ensure that an offender with many previous convictions does not receive a sentence above the normal range of sentences appropriate for the present offence. The notion of a "ceiling" for the offence thus places a limit on the importance attached to the repetition of conduct by asserting that the overall penalty should be proportional to the gravity of the conduct manifested in the present offence.

30. For a useful account of the present and previous law see Wasik, 1993, Ch. 6 and Appendix 1.

31. The pre-Criminal Justice Act 1991 approach involved observing the following principles (see Thomas, 1979):

1) The first consideration for a sentencer contemplating imposition of a fine was whether the offence and surrounding circumstances required the imposition of a custodial sentence. The 1991 Act is silent on this but probably seriousness determines if a fine is appropriate in principle. It was considered wrong in principle to impose a heavy fine on a wealthy man in a case where a person of less substantial means would normally be sentenced to imprisonment. It was also wrong in principle to impose a custodial sentence on someone just because he lacked the means to pay a fine; *McGowan*, (1974).

2) Given that the offence was not one which required the imposition of a custodial sentence the second step was to determine the *level* of fine appropriate to the offence. Again, it was wrong in principle to increase the amount of the fine where the offender was unusually affluent, as in *R v Fairbairn* (1980). Section 18 (1) of the 1991 Act

requires the Court to inquire into an offender's financial circumstances before fixing the *level* of a fine.

3) Where a sentencer had determined that the offence did not require a custodial sentence and that the facts of the case considered in the abstract would justify a fine of a given amount, the next question was whether the proposed fine could be *paid* by the offender within a reasonable time. At this stage means would be investigated and the amount appropriate to the offence considered in the abstract would be reduced, where necessary, to an amount which offender could realistically be expected to pay. Section 18 (2) of the 1991 Act requires that the amount of fine must reflect the court's view of the seriousness of the offence. Section 18 (3) requires courts to take into account the circumstances of the case including the financial circumstances of the defendant in fixing the *amount* of fine. Finally, Section 18 (5) makes it clear that a fine can be increased as well as reduced when the court takes the financial circumstances of the defendant into account under S18 (3). It is unclear from the provisions where the balance between seriousness and financial circumstances lies (see further Wasik, pp. 87, 214).

32. *The Times*, 9 February 1994.

33. For a summary of the present law see Wasik and Taylor, 1995, p. 16.

34. See in particular the Tom Sargant Memorial Lecture delivered by Lord Taylor C.J. in January 1994 and *The Times,* 12 and 24 April 1994.

35. In his speech to NACRO, November 1993.

36. In a speech delivered to the New Assembly of Churches, London. The following extracts indicate the extent of his displeasure with the direction of Government penal policy;

"The easy option, which has a miserable record of failure, is to send more and more people to prison regardless of the consequences including the shocking waste of resources which could be spent elsewhere. The difficult option is to try to identify the underlying causes of criminal conduct and then to set about tackling those causes.

I appreciate that you may say it is hardly up to you, a judge, to complain about prison overcrowding. Who sends people to prison but the judges? That is of course true, but they do so in the context which the Government and Parliament acts. My concern is that that context is in the process of change and that there is a fashion not confined to the totally uninformed to indulge in rhetoric advocating increased sentences across the board in ways which will be counterproductive."

37. See, for example, *The Times*, 19 and 20 January, 3 February 1994.
38. See, for example, the essay by Shirley Williams in *The Times*, 14 February 1994.

2 Drug Offences

1 Introduction

This chapter describes how English sentencing law has initiated a reversal of the welfarist approach to the treatment of drug offenders contained in recent criminal justice legislation. The argument is illustrated by examining the nature of the false dichotomy which exists between custody and treatment created by recent sentencing law which promotes retributive rather than rehabilitative sentencing objectives. Relevant provisions and principles contained in the Criminal Justice Acts 1991 and 1993 are analysed and comparison made between Court of Appeal sentencing principles and Magistrates' Association sentencing guidelines for drug offences which confirms the trend towards more punitive sentencing in an increasingly retributivist penal climate. The courts continue to deal with the symptoms rather than the causes of drug offending with neither the executive nor the judiciary able to contribute towards the development of a coherent sentencing strategy for dealing with drug related crime. It is suggested that the solution may be to introduce strategic incentives to treatment in the criminal process.

2 A bifurcation of approach

English sentencing policy for drug offenders has failed to establish an effective rationale from drawing a distinction between repressive and therapeutic objectives which is reflected in sentencing law. Recent criminal legislation on drug control has consistently fostered the prevailing myth that there is a clear distinction to be drawn between drug-takers and drug-pushers or suppliers with regard to the scaling of penalties. As Collison points out, the reality is that once problem drug users are drawn into the criminal justice system, they rapidly assume the status of suppliers and traffickers rather than victims (Collison, 1993, p. 38, 1994, p. 25). The dividing line between the two groups clearly drawn in the legislative provisions is in reality blurred and in a constant state of flux. Hence, punitive and deterrent measures designed only for the so-called "villains" are in fact applied to both groups. It should also be borne in mind that the largest prisoner group relates to Class B drug offenders rather than Class A suppliers and traffickers who continue to elude the courts (Home Office, 1992). It appears, therefore, that the legislative provisions are failing to reach the most serious Class A drug offenders.

The blurring of the distinction between the requirements of custody and treatment for drug offenders has profound implications. First, it results in the criminalisation of less serious offenders with consequential increases in drug-related criminal activity and its attendant social consequences. This should prompt a re-assessment of sentencing policy for drug offenders in Government legislation which has so far failed to materialise. There is no doubt that many recidivist drug offenders become locked in a cycle of increased prisonisation exacerbated by a sentencing approach which fails to take account of the serious nature of the prison drug problem. Secondly, the confused relationship between custody and treatment within penal institutions inevitably results in the dilution of treatment initiatives. There is a tendency for treatment programmes to become diluted within the mainstream prison system since specialised programmes designed for specialist institutions tend to fail when applied elsewhere - it is their specialisation which ensures their success. It is also clearly recognised that any form of compulsory treatment is invariably defined as punishment by prison inmates. It is not realistic or possible to treat someone who does not wish to be treated. In such a situation inmates submitting to voluntary treatment have to define themselves as "sick" i.e. admit they have a problem (this effectively amounts to self-labelling). Experience of prison treatment programmes indicates high expectations of inmates voluntarily requesting treatment from trained staff within the institution. A situation of total dependency may develop so the result is that inmates either want no input from treatment staff or total input. Treatment failure can therefore be significantly counter-productive as leading to resentment and increased withdrawal from co-operation. Such an outcome is a distinct possibility where the inmates' problems originate from outside the prison and where treatment inside the prison will not remove the cause(s). This is particularly appropriate in respect of those social conditions related to drug offences. Hence, many related issues are prison induced. Finally, it should also be remembered that treatment within an institution may become a guise for control. A significant treatment programme necessarily conflicts with custodial objectives since the objectives of treatment and custody are mutually contradictory. Treatment inevitably means that individualised criteria will be applied to inmates which may be perceived as "special" favours or privileges by other inmates. It is therefore impossible to accept any system of specialised treatment which does not explicitly recognise that inmates must contribute to the maintenance of the prison. The endemic nature of the drug culture in British prisons[1] and the power hierarchy it sustains exacerbates attempts to foster individual or group treatment programmes.

The continued emphasis on punishment and deterrence is clearly discernible in recent legislation aimed at curbing drug trafficking (Sallon and Bedingfield, 1993). Although such developments are understandable their introduction has been at the expense of a diminution of offenders' due process rights. There are three major erosions of due process discernible in the Drug Trafficking Act 1994.[2] The first concerns the power of a court to require the defendant to provide such information as is specified in the confiscation order within a specified time (S12). Section 12 (5) provides that if the defendant fails, without reasonable excuse, to comply with the order the court may draw such inferences from that failure as it considers appropriate. This is tantamount to the abolition of any right of silence in this context. Secondly, S2 (8) reverses the rule in *R v Dickens* (1990) by providing that the standard of proof required to determine any question as to whether a person has benefited from drug trafficking or the amount to be recovered. Thirdly, S2 (2) reverses the Court of Appeal's decision in *R v Redbourne* (1992) by making the assumptions[3] under the Act mandatory. Section 4 (4) provides that the court shall not make any required assumption if that assumption is shown to be incorrect in the defendant's case or the court is satisfied that there would be a serious risk of injustice in the defendant's case if the assumption were to be made. Thomas suggests that should the defendant challenge any required assumption the prosecution would then be put to proof according to the civil standard on the issue of whether the defendant owned the relevant property or made the alleged expenditure (Thomas, 1994c, p. 96). If this was established the onus would then be on the defendant to establish otherwise, again according to the civil standard. If the defendant failed to discharge this burden the court would be required to assume that the property or expenditure was connected with

31

drug trafficking, unless it was satisfied that there would be a serious risk of injustice in the defendant's case if the assumption were made (S4 (4) (b)). Sallon and Bedingfield (1993) question the efficacy of a policy which drastically erodes some of the fundamental rights of an accused in a criminal trial without establishing the potential for any perceptible reduction in drug use. The laudable objective of depriving drug dealers of profits does not in their view justify such an attack on due process rights since it cannot be assumed that drug use will be significantly curtailed simply as a consequence of attempting to eliminate dealers' profits (Sallon and Bedingfield, 1993, p. 172). However, this argument can be countered by the utilitarian view that even a minimal reduction in drug use justifies the erosion of due process rights where vulnerable drug victims are concerned.

3   The Criminal Justice Acts 1991 and 1993

Both drug specific and general recent criminal justice legislation demonstrate that confusion in policy objectives has facilitated the trend towards retributivist drug sentencing practice. Paradoxically, the Criminal Justice Act 1991 was heralded as evidence of a significant policy change in the sentencing of drug offenders (Collison, 1993, p. 385) with the introduction of a requirement to be added to a standard probation order that an offender should receive treatment with a view to the reduction or elimination of the offender's dependency on drugs or alcohol (Schedule 1, Part II, para. 6 (2)). It is important to note that para. 6 (1) not only makes it a condition of such an order that the offender is dependant on drugs or alcohol but also that his dependency caused or contributed to the offence in respect of which the probation order is made (para. 6 (1) (a) and (b)).[4] The drug or alcohol dependency must be treatable (para. 6 (1) (c)). Prior to the introduction of the 1991 Act provisions in October 1992 there were three alternative treatment-oriented sentencing options available in the case of drug offenders following appropriate assessment. The first of these, a probation order containing a requirement as to psychiatric treatment, was available where the offender was not found to be suffering from one of the forms of mental disorder which would have justified the making of a hospital order.[5]   It was recognised that such an order was appropriate where it was felt that the order would have such beneficial effects on the offender as would outweigh the risk to the public; *R v Mcdonald* (1983). The other two pre-1991 Act probation orders were orders made with a residential requirement in a drug rehabilitation unit or as directed by a probation officer. The 1991 Act provisions preserved the residential option but made treatment as a non-resident available as directed by a probation officer (para. 3). The most significant aspect of the changed criteria relates to the wide definition of drug dependency as including a propensity towards the misuse of drugs or alcohol, thus moving away from the restrictive psychiatric requirement (para. 6 (9)). The tenor of the provisions certainly indicates a more pragmatic and welfarist approach to drug treatment rather than crime control and it would appear that drug agencies were advised to regard the 1991 Act's approach as a major policy initiative requiring significant forward planning. Lee observes that the Act's provisions fail to provide a clear community based sentencing alternative for recidivist drug offenders and further reports a view that sentencers may prefer the pre-Act conditional residence requirement rather than conditional treatment since the former can be used as a punitive restriction on liberty (Lee, 1993). These comments indicate a need to clarify the position of conditional treatment for drug offenders in the range of community sentences.

Notwithstanding, there is no doubt that the overriding policy contribution of the 1991 Act was its emphasis on just deserts.[6] Subsequent amendment of S1 by S66 Criminal Justice Act 1993 was, however, evidence of a concerted re-alignment of policy towards punishment and deterrence with major repercussions for the criminal justice system as a whole. In essence the amended S1 removed the controversial restriction that the courts were only allowed to take account of the offence and one other associated offence in considering whether to impose a custodial sentence or a community penalty on the basis of its seriousness. Section 66 (2) made corresponding amendments to allow a court to consider all associated offences when determining the length of a custodial sentence. Finally, S66 (3) amended S3 (3) (a) of the 1991 Act by requiring that, in forming an opinion as to whether a custodial sentence is justified and as to the length of any such sentence, the court must take into account all such information as is available to it about the offence and any associated offences combined with it under SS1 (2) (a) or 2 (2) (a) (as amended). These provisions then marked the end of a deliberate sentencing policy aimed at diverting the small scale recidivist offender away from custodial to community based sentencing alternatives. In particular, it ensured a return to punishment at the expense of treatment for the majority of drug offenders. As if to compound these difficulties an amended S29 (1) provides "in considering the seriousness of any offence the court may take into account any previous convictions of the offender or any failure of his to respond to previous sentences". Thomas has argued that since S3 (3) impliedly forbids a court from considering information about the offender (rather than the offence)

33

when considering seriousness all but the actual circumstances of the offence must be ignored (Thomas, 1993a). This would mean that although the offender's previous convictions (viz. the fact of them) would be relevant the behaviour or individual circumstances i.e. the causes of the original offence would not be. This would clearly be a serious omission in the court's ability to deal satisfactorily with drug offenders. As Collison points out the drug user who lacks the motivation to give up and who has demonstrated this through his past criminal behaviour may become a suitable case for prison more quickly (Collison, 1993, pp. 390, 393). Furthermore, there are many drug related offences involving recidivists where their drug-related nature remains undisclosed due to the perceived narrow range of realistic alternatives available to them. It is perceived that strict breach and treatment conditions with forced intervention make the custodial option the least unattractive.

It is significant that the Criminal Justice Act 1991 was responsible for the introduction of a substantially progressive provision concerning mentally abnormal offenders in S4 which provides that in addition to requiring a medical report in all cases where an offender is or appears to be mentally disordered (unless the court deems it unnecessary), the court must also consider the likely effect of a custodial sentence on any mental condition and treatment that may be available. However, the requirement to obtain a medical report does not apply where a pre-sentence report has been dispensed with under S3 (2) (as amended by Schedule 9, para. 40 Criminal Justice and Public Order Act 1994) on the basis that the court is of the opinion that it is unnecessary to obtain one in the circumstances of the case. Nevertheless, it is arguable that the provisions of S4 should be extended to drug offenders generally[7] as regards the necessity to consider the likely effect of a custodial sentence on the offender's drug problem and treatment availability. At present, unless the drug offender is specifically selected by the court for one of the treatment-oriented options previously discussed, he or she will be subject to the general provisions contained in the 1991 Act, if the offence is so serious that it merits a custodial sentence in any event. Therefore, if a pre-sentence report is obtained, the court is only under an obligation to take into account the content of the report, together with any other relevant information about the offender and the offence, including aggravating and mitigating factors. The power to mitigate a sentence in the circumstances of the case is retained by S28 but the provisions do not oblige the court to consider the impact of imprisonment on the offender's condition. This is clearly an important omission.

It is arguable that the early release procedures introduced by the Criminal Justice Act 1991[8] may result in longer terms of imprisonment being served by drug offenders in common with offenders in general. As Thomas has pointed out, those offenders serving medium term sentences (from twelve months to three years) who would have had the best chance of early release on licence under the previous system have in principle to serve considerably longer sentences under the 1991 Act and are also subject to the mandatory recall provisions (Thomas, 1992). The attention of the judiciary was drawn to these dangers by Lord Taylor's Practice Statement on the Criminal Justice Act 1991 made on 1 October, 1992 to coincide with the Act's implementation. The significance of the direction was that it reversed a long-standing sentencing convention against a court referring to questions of remission (abolished by the 1991 Act) or parole in deciding the appropriate sentence. It is, as yet, impossible to gauge the effect (if any) of this important change in sentencing policy on sentence lengths. It is also arguable that the strict breach criteria introduced by the 1991 Act for community service and probation orders will result in an increase in custodial sentences for drug offenders where drug dependency renders them more likely to commit breaches of such orders (see Collison, 1993, p. 393).

Provided an offender's offence justifies a custodial sentence under S1 (2) (a) of the 1991 Act, S1 (2) (b) introduced a protective element to be added to the sentence in the case of violent and sexual offences (defined by S31 (1)) where necessary to protect the public from serious harm from the offender. At present, S31 (3) states that any reference to protecting the public from serious harm is to be construed as a reference to protecting members of the public from death or serious personal injury, whether physical or psychological which would be occasioned by future violent or sexual offences committed by the offender. It would suggest that there is a case for extending the scope of this provision to drug suppliers and drug pushers. In *R v Bowler* (1993) the Court of Appeal recognised that in assessing the possibility of future serious harm a court may have regard to the degree of vulnerability of potential victims and it is certainly arguable that the definition of serious harm contained in S31 (3) is capable of including such harm as is caused by the supply and sale of dangerous drugs. Since there is no definition of "dangerousness" and no legal test or guidance in its prediction contained in the 1991 Act, or elsewhere, it is open to suggest that the danger presented by drug suppliers/pushers approximates that of an imminent danger (see Walker, 1985, p. 363) against which the public require protection. There would be no difficulty in accommodating the danger in terms of the sorts of harm against which precautions are justifiable in the terms postulated by Floud and Young (1981).[9] The change required would be rather in terms of the behaviour which produces the harms in question. The necessity for this proposed sentencing change stems from the inadequacy of the life sentence as the maximum for serious Class A supply cases as a protective measure although it is recognised that the protective efficiency of sentences under S1 (2) (b) is currently limited by the upper limit of the maximum term available for the offence (Thomas, 1993c). This problem could be remedied by the introduction of an indeterminate second part to the double-track sentence which although intended for society's protection is subject to obligatory reviews with the onus of justification remaining with those desiring the continued detention of the offender.

4   The Magistrates' Association Sentencing Guidelines

A comparison of Court of Appeal sentencing principles and Magistrates' Association Sentencing Guidelines for drug offences provides further evidence of a prospective increase in punitive sentences for drug offenders. The introduction of revised sentencing guidelines for magistrates in September 1993 was widely treated with some suspicion that the courts would be reluctant to depart from the prescribed "entry points" to take account of factors relevant to the seriousness of the offence and mitigating factors.[10] It was felt that the new guidelines would result in an increase in the prison population because of a fundamental change in their recommended approach to sentencing. Under the former guidelines (issued June 1992) there were a number of "starting points" for each offence and magistrates were invited to move forward to consider tougher sentences on the basis of weighing up aggravating and mitigating factors and rejecting lesser alternatives. The new guidelines provide that the term "entry point" is simply used as a guide for an offence of "average" seriousness (page 3) but the criticism is that the entry points have been fixed at a high level in the case of certain offences and that magistrates will be deterred from considering lesser alternatives as they would have been forced to do by the approach adopted in the former guidelines.

Detailed guidelines for drug offences were laid down by Lord Lane C.J. in *R v Aramah* (1982) and *R v Bilinski* (1987). In *Aramah* Lord Lane distinguished between Class A drugs such as heroin, morphine and cocaine and Class B drugs, such as cannabis. For importation of Class A drugs sentences could range up to 14 years depending on the street value of the drugs.[11] This maximum was increased to life imprisonment by the

Controlled Drugs (Penalties) Act 1985. Both the National Mode of Trial Guidelines (1990) and the new Magistrates' Association Sentencing Guidelines (page 22) make it clear that such cases should normally be committed to the Crown Court for trial.[12] Similarly, in the case of possession of Class A drugs with intent to supply there is general agreement between *Aramah*, the National Mode of Trial Guidelines and the new Magistrates' Association Sentencing Guidelines on the need for Crown Court committal. In *Aramah* it was suggested that it would depend on the individual circumstances of the offender but in many cases deprivation of liberty would be the appropriate penalty with sentences of three to four years commonplace; *R v Faluade* (1989). In *R v Kempley* (1994) Russell L.J. in the Court of Appeal emphasised that there had to be a deterrent element in any sentence imposed on someone found in possession of the Class A drug ecstacy with intent to supply. A five year prison sentence was thus described as not wrong in principle, and not too long, although heavy for a first offender. In the case of simple possession of Class A drugs Lord Lane in *Aramah* suggested that the possible variety of individual circumstances was so wide that it was not possible to lay down any meaningful guidelines but that custody would be "both proper and expedient" in many cases. Simple possession for personal use has attracted sentences in the range six to 12 months in recent years; e.g. *R v Gallagher* (1990). However, although the National Mode of Trial Guidelines advocate that possession of Class A drugs cases should be committed for trial unless the amount is small and consistent only with personal use, the new Magistrates' Association Sentencing Guidelines (page 23) recommend the entry point as a community penalty. The former Magistrates' Association Guidelines (page 22) starting point for possession of a small quantity was a guideline fine of 30 units (under the now abolished unit fine system). If the critics are proved correct the sentencing level in such cases will be raised since the existence of the entry point will dissuade magistrates from considering lesser alternatives such as the fine and they will be more inclined to move up the penal severity scale. Justification of the reverse will become more difficult. It may also be the case that magistrates will simply fail to take proper account of those factors which might make an offence less serious or neglect those factors relevant to personal mitigation which are crucial in many drug offence cases.

In cases involving possession of a Class B drug with intent to supply the sentence level will normally depend on the circumstances such as the scale of the operation and the significance of the offender in the chain of supply. If there is no commercial motive for the offence it is unlikely that a custodial sentence will be regarded as appropriate; *R v Spiers* (1985). In Class B possession cases there is a consensus between the National Mode of Trial Guidelines and both the new and former Magistrates' Association Sentencing Guidelines regarding the necessity for committal unless there was only small scale supply for no payment. However, the new Guidelines recommend the entry point as custody for cases not committed for trial although indicating the existence of a small amount as a factor which may justify the court's decision that the offence is not so serious that only a custodial sentence is appropriate. It is also possible that the court may find that in such circumstances an offence is serious enough for a community penalty but it is only at the third seriousness level that compensation, discharge or a fine are possibly appropriate. It, therefore, requires a decisive move downwards from the entry point to achieve what was indicated as the starting point under the former Guidelines (page 24) for small scale supply of Class B drugs with no payment, viz. a fine. The former Guidelines thus required a decisive move upwards to reach the next seriousness level and eventually reaching the custody threshold (page 23).

Where the offence is simple possession of Class B drugs a fine is usually considered appropriate; *R v Jones* (1981). Both the former and new Magistrates' Association Sentencing Guidelines (pages 24 and 25 respectively) reflect agreement on the appropriateness of a fine in such cases although, as the National Mode of Trial Guidelines point out, possession cases should be committed for trial where the quantity was substantial. General principles have established that continued flouting of the law may justify a short prison sentence; *R v Robertson, Coupar and Baxendale* (1982), and even possession of a small amount may result in a short custodial sentence where the offender has a persistent record of cannabis related offences; *R v Osborne* (1982). The dominant trend is simple possession cases is towards release with a caution thus reflecting a trend towards general relaxation of penalties for soft drug use in European countries; for example, Germany (Constitutional Court decision, 28 April 1994). It is interesting to note that some 16 per cent of Germans aged between 12 and 39 admit to having consumed illegal drugs at least once (cannabis predominating). Findings from the 1992 British Crime Survey reveal that some 28 per cent of UK citizens in the 16 to 29 age group admit to some drug use (again, cannabis predominating) (Home Office, 1993). Nevertheless, although 24 per cent admitted cannabis use this fell to 1 per cent for those aged 12 to 13 admitting cannabis use in 1991.[13] It is consequently apparent that *de facto* de-criminalization of soft drug use and possession has occurred in certain European countries without necessitating deliberate sentencing policy changes.[14]

The comments made earlier regarding the effect of the amended S29 Criminal Justice Act 1991 are equally pertinent in the case of the new Magistrates' Association Guidelines which specifically include the existence of previous convictions and failure to respond to previous sentences (if relevant) as factors justifying an increase in the seriousness level for the offence. Ashworth and Gibson have recently suggested that one implication of the new S29 (1) may extend to the inclusion within the meaning of a "response" of behaviour which may fall short of criminality or a conviction (Ashworth and Gibson, 1994, p. 105).[15] As indicated, this may, if correct, further disadvantage drug offenders with their notoriously erratic patterns of co-operation with criminal justice agencies.

The weakness of recent Government drug sentencing policy was sharply illustrated in adverse reaction to the proposal to increase the maximum fines for cannabis possession fivefold to £2500 by an amendment to the Criminal Justice and Public Order Bill (1993). Fines for illegal possession, production and supply of amphetamines were also to be increased from £500 to £2500.[16] Predictably, the surprise announcement was justified by reference to the Government's "get tough" approach to law and order so that individuals found guilty of such offences would feel the impact and realise the consequences of the fine instead of viewing it with indifference.[17] Moves towards liberalisation were considered inappropriate notwithstanding that recent Home Office statistics showed that over 50 per cent of those arrested for cannabis possession received a caution. The obvious implication of the proposals, echoed by police and legal opinion, would be a huge increase in those receiving custodial sentences through inability to pay increased fines.

5   A return to welfarism

It has been argued that the therapeutic considerations contained in the Criminal Justice Act 1991 appear doomed by the general climate of punishment and deterrence now evident in recent Government sentencing policy. In the medium to long term recent changes will neither reduce drug use nor the imprisonment of drug offenders. It is submitted that strategic sentencing alternatives adopted in certain European countries would repay closer scrutiny and provide constructive alternatives.

Italian criminal policy on drug abuse provides an example of recent innovative changes in sentencing policy (Coluccia and Marzi, 1991). Prior to 1990 Italian policy was characterised by a general discriminalisation of drug use for personal consumption but sentencing structures failed to provide precise incentives to seek treatment. The new law n 162 of 26 June 1990 marked a definite philosophical change by asserting that it was a crime to take drugs of whatever type. As Coluccia and Marzi state this was achieved by changing drug taking from a situation attributable to a specific personal interest to one firmly in the public domain subject to State sanction and control mechanisms (page 2). In other words, the 1990 law re-asserted the State's commitment to combat drug abuse but, more importantly, to pursue the criminological causes responsible for the situation. The Italian law contains elements of repressiveness with a commitment to provide incentives for the drug offender to seek treatment. For example, in the case of a detainee guilty of soft drug abuse the Prefect may formally invite the detainee to desist and carries the responsibility for primary prevention. Repeated violations carry further obligations on the State's authority to seek to prevent further violation. Admission to any treatment or therapeutic programme is, however, subject to personal request at the discretion of the Prefect. If the detainee fails to comply in certain specified ways[18] with the therapeutic programme the Prefect may refer the case to the State Prosecutor for further action.

One important aspect of the Italian system is that once the addicted offender has submitted to voluntary treatment the responsibility for the therapeutic programme becomes the sole concern of the Public Health Service which is under a legal obligation to report[19] to the Prefect. The choice between punishment and cure may, however, result in indirect coercion of the offender since the entire therapeutic process is against a background of control. These difficulties can only be completely circumvented in the case of drug addicts who voluntarily submit to treatment outside the prosecution context. The procedure does, nevertheless, provide an example of how the criminal process can provide strategic incentives to seek therapeutic alternatives where the boundaries between custody and treatment are clearly delineated.[20]

Apart from interventionist approaches based on voluntary submission to treatment Italian law also provides for treatment-oriented sentencing alternatives whereby the addicted offender may serve his sentence in a public or private therapeutic community provided he has been sentenced to a period of detention of less than three years and the offences are related to the drug addiction. There is also provision for the relevant court to suspend the sentence for five years if the offender has either already arranged, or, is in the process of undergoing, a therapeutic programme.

In contrast to the Italian system, the German system relies more substantially on the notion of treatment incentives for sentencing addicted offenders (Council of Europe Report, 1991, p. 54). The most important legal provisions relate to the nature of the sentence. Section 56 of the Criminal Code provides that in the case of custodial sentences of up to one year (exceptionally up to two years) a sentence may be suspended on probation for two to five years if the court is satisfied that the offender will not re-offend, notwithstanding a prison sentence. Conditions may be imposed as to therapeutic treatment with consent of the offender. Failure to respond results in revocation of the suspension. A constructive provision in S57 of the Criminal Code allows the suspension of the remaining part of a sentence after two-thirds (exceptionally one-half) has been served if the court is satisfied that the offender will not re-offend provided he shows a willingness to undergo therapy. Further possibilities exist under SS35 and 36 of the Narcotics Act, where a sentence is not suspended (due to unfavourable treatment prognosis), for the public prosecutor, with the court's consent, to postpone execution of a prison sentence (or the remainder of one of not more than two years) for up to two years where a person convicted of committing an offence related to drug addition is undergoing treatment or is definitely about to commence it. The duration of the treatment counts towards the sentence, and successful therapy may result in suspension of the sentence and possibly remission of the sentence. Failure to complete the therapy may result in revocation of sentence postponement and continued execution of the sentence, although renewed postponement is a possibility. In common with the Italian procedure, German drug sentencing law not only reflects a clear distinction between repressive and therapeutic measures it also integrates therapy into the sentencing process and uses it as an incentive enabling the offender to mitigate or suspend the punitive aspects of the sentence.

Lesser used alternatives in Germany allow the public prosecutor to refrain from bringing a charge (with the court's consent) provided the accused proves that he has been undergoing treatment for addiction for at least three months. This provision is subject to an expected prison sentence of at least two years and proceedings may be discontinued after four years provided treatment has been completed, no further offences have been committed, and, no new facts have emerged which might result in a more severe sentence for the original offence. Finally, S64 of the Criminal Code allows a court to order in a sentence for admission of an addicted offender to an institution for drug addicts if the prognosis is that he may commit serious offences in the future because of his disposition.

41

6   Implications for U.K. sentencing policy

The relative merits of voluntary and compulsory treatment of addicted offenders as replacing or complementing criminal sanctions is outside the scope of this discussion and there are many examples of each approach adopted by different jurisdictions (see Council of Europe Report, 1991, p. 27). The main concern of this chapter has been with the consequences of accepting the treatment principle on the formulation of sentencing policy and legislation. It has been argued that the United Kingdom is in the process of abandoning the limited welfarism of the 1991 Criminal Justice Act for increasing repression and criminalisation of addicted offenders and drug-related crime. Clearly, prevention and repression needs to be complemented with therapeutic considerations and, whilst the argument between compulsory treatment and voluntary treatment hinges on the motivation of the drug addict, I would argue that a compromise solution must be urgently pursued. This compromise, essentially, represents a reduction in penalty levels, and implementation of suspended sentences and strategic postponement in sentence execution provided therapeutic measures are completed.[21] This provides system inducements not inconsistent with due process in addition to personal motivation with the former likely to increase the probability of the latter being sustained to achieve a successful outcome. In formulating legislative proposals the executive should take into account the meaning of drug use and its effects both in terms of explaining behaviour and responses to treatment (see Parker, 1993, p. 3). It cannot be correct to pursue a policy of repressive law enforcement which ignores the causes which may lead individuals to use and abuse drugs.[22]

References

1. Maden et al (1991) estimated that 11 per cent of the imprisoned male population and approximately 25 per cent of the female population were dependent on drugs whilst it was acknowledged that a significant number of imprisoned drug users do not admit their problem to the prison medical service. Sections 152 and 153 Criminal Justice and Public Order Act 1994 provided powers for prison officers to test for drugs in prisons and search for unauthorised property. *The Guardian*, 7 July 1994, reported that random drug tests would be imposed on 12,000 prisons annually following a prison service survey revealing a 58 per cent increase in Class A drug use in nine prisons the previous year. Five per cent would receive random tests and 5 per cent on suspicion.

2. See Thomas (1994) for a detailed exposition of the changes brought about by the Criminal Justice Act 1993. The Drug Trafficking Act 1994 came into force on 3 February 1995 and consolidated the Drug Trafficking Offences Act 1986 (and subsequent amendments). It brought into force the new provisions concerning the confiscation of drug trafficking proceeds which had previously been contained in Part II of the Criminal Justice Act 1993.

3. Section 4 (3) provides the required assumptions are:
   (a) that any property appearing to the court -
       (i) to have been held by the defendant at any time since his conviction, or
       (ii) to have been transferred to him at any time since the beginning of the period of six years ending when the proceedings were instituted against him, was received by him, at the earliest time at which he appears to the court to have held it, as a payment or reward in connection with drug trafficking carried on by him,
   (b) that any expenditure of his since the beginning of that period was met out of payments received in connection with drug trafficking carried on by him, and
   (c) that, for the purpose of valuing any property received or assumed to have been received by him at any time as such a reward, he received the property free from any other interests in it.

43

4. It is interesting to compare the position of mentally abnormal offenders where the making of a hospital order may be appropriate when no causal link has been established between the offender's mental disorder and the offence in respect of which the order is made; *R v McBride* (1972). It would seem that the protectionist provision S1 (2) (b) applies to either drug or mentally abnormal offenders on the basis that there is a predicted possibility of serious harm being caused in the future without any regard as to whether there has been a record of serious harm in the past; see *R v Bowler* (1993), *R v Williams* (1993), *R v Apelt* (1994).

5. Such an order can now require the offender to submit to treatment by or under the direction of a chartered psychologist (in addition to medical practitioner) for his mental condition; Schedule 9, para. 10, Criminal Justice and Public Order Act 1994. Note, however, that the evidence of a "duly qualified medical practitioner" is still required under S12 Mental Health Act 1983 for a psychiatric probation order to be made by the court. This would appear to exclude the evidence of a chartered psychologist.

6. This philosophical change was made explicit by the Government in the 1990 White Paper (para. 1.6).

7. I.e. not restricted by the definition of "drug dependency" contained in the Act.

8. These confined parole to those sentenced to four years or more imprisonment. Where sentenced to less than four years, the Secretary of State may release on licence at the half-way stage, but, if between such release and the end of the period covered by the original sentence, the offender commits an imprisonable offence he may be recalled to serve the balance of the original sentence outstanding at the time of the fresh offence. Where sentenced to a four year or more determinate sentence prisoners are released on licence after serving two-thirds of their sentence and become eligible for parole at the half-way stage. Prisoners remain at risk following release in the same way as short term prisoners.

9. Viz "any offence which caused or was intended to cause; death; serious bodily injury; serious sexual assault; severe or prolonged pain or mental distress; loss or damage to property which results in severe personal hardship; damage to the environment which has serious adverse effects on public health or safety, serious damage to the security of the state."

10. For example, see comments by Roger Ede, Secretary to the Law Society's Criminal Law Committee and Frances Crook, Director of the Howard League in *"The Gazette"* 22 September 1993, p. 4. Scepticism was also voiced by the Lord Chief Justice, Lord Taylor, in his speech to NACRO in November 1993.

11. It was decided in *R v Aroyewumi and Ors* (1994) that street values would no longer be used as a basis for determining the sentence in cases of importation of Class A controlled drugs such as heroin and cocaine. A better way to measure the relative significance of any seizure of Class A drugs is by weight. On the question of purity see *R v Patel and Varshney* (1994).

12. Note that S44 Criminal Justice and Public Order Act 1994 abolishes committal proceedings in SS4-8 Magistrates Courts Act 1980 with a new transfer for trial procedure detailed in Schedule 4 of the 1994 Act.

13. These figures are supported by research carried out by Leitner, Shapland and Wiles (1993), which confirmed (*inter alia*) that:-
    (i) only a small minority of the population admitted ever taking illicit drugs
    (ii) there were regional variations in admitted drug use in addition to variations by drug type
    (iii) "recent" usage was much less extensive than "ever" usage
    (iv) drug usage was spread generally across different social classes
    (v) generally, whites were more likely than non-whites to have used illicit drugs
    (vi) men were more likely than women to have taken illicit drugs

14. Apart from police cautioning practices for soft drug use (and even small amounts of hard drugs (e.g. heroin) for personal use in certain cities) experimental Arrest Referral Schemes have been established in certain areas. For example, the Southwark project referred some 76 drug users during its two year existence with two-thirds having been arrested for non-drug offences.

15. For a contrary view see Wasik and von Hirsch (1994).

16. Announced by the Home Secretary in February 1994. Schedule 8, Part II, Criminal Justice and Public Order Act 1994 contained (*inter alia*) increases in maximum fines for offences relating to possession of Class B drugs (S5 (2) and Schedule 4, column 5, Misuse of Drugs Act 1971) from £500 to £2500 and offences

relating to the possession of Class C drugs (S5 (2) and Schedule 4, column 6, Misuse of Drugs Act 1971) from £200 to £1000 applying to offences committed after 3 February 1995; The Criminal Justice and Public Order Act 1994 (Commencement No. 5) Order 1994.

17. A source close to Mr Howard was quoted as saying: "People who transgress should realise they face a fine, not a minor financial penalty they can view as an occupational overhead", *"The Sunday Times"* 13 February 1994.

18. Viz: 1) the offender does not appear before the Prefect;
    2) the offender openly refuses the therapeutic programme
    3) the offender interrupts the programme without justification.

19. According to art. 123 the report must deal with the following points:-
    (1) course of the programme
    (2) behaviour of the individual with regard to the programme
    (3) results obtained following completion of the programme "in terms of cessation of drug taking".

20. Solivetti has recently analysed the failure of increases in penal sanctions for drug traffickers and the re-introduction of indirect sanctions involving therapy and rehabilitation to deal with the alarming recent increases in drug-taking and drug-related crime in Italian society. This failure is manifest in a widespread lack of belief in the effectiveness of the policy and suspicion that the rationale for increasing sanctions lies in the political value of governmental response to public reaction (Solivetti, 1994).

21. See the conclusions of the Council of Europe Report (1991), p. 35.

22. *The Times*, 3 June 1994 reported that the prison population in the United States had almost tripled the 1980 figure at nearly one million. U.S. Bureau of Justice Statistics attributed almost half the increase to the U.S. Government's war on drugs with stiffer sentences and limits on parole.

3 White Collar Crime

The aim of this chapter is two-fold. First, it examines the suggestions and recommendations of the Royal Commission on Criminal Justice (1993) relating to the trial of fraud cases and assesses their significance. Secondly, the sentencing of white collar offenders[1] is considered in the light of the Criminal Justice Acts (1991) and (1993), recent guidance provided by the Court of Appeal (Criminal Division) and the Royal Commission's proposals. The impact of these developments on both the theoretical and practical notions of criminal justice in the trial and sentencing of white collar offenders is also addressed.

1 The Trial

Procedure
The most controversial recommendation made by the Royal Commission was undoubtedly the proposal that in either way offences the defendant should no longer have a right to insist on trial by jury. (Royal Commision on Criminal Justice, 1993, Ch. 6, para. 113). The arguments against the proposal are well-rehearsed amd essentially amount to the idea that individual rights and due process would be sacrificed to the demands of bureaucratic expediency. Although not immediately evident, in practical terms a number of white collar offences appear affected by this proposal, such as theft in breach of trust (S1 Theft Act, 1968), certain offences relating to companies such as fraudulent trading (S458 Companies Act 1985) and offences involving banking and financial services such as insider dealing on the Stock Exchange (S52 Criminal Justice Act, 1993). The National Mode of Trial Guidelines issued by Lord Lane in 1990[2], whilst not

dealing with offences involving companies, banking or financial services, refer to theft and fraud and recommend summary trial unless the magistrates' court considered that a particular case had one or more of the following features and that its sentencing powers were insufficient; (1) Breach of trust by person in position of substantial authority or in whom a high degree of trust was placed (2) Committed or disguised in a sophisticated manner (3) Committed by an organised gang. (4) A particularly vulnerable victim, for example, the elderly or infirm (5) Unrecovered property of high value. The Magistrates' Association Sentencing Guidelines[3] refer to the Mode of Trial Guidelines and list a number of seriousness indicators which may be taken into account by Magistrates in reaching their decision.[4] These factors are similar to those described in the Mode of Trial Guidelines. The likelihood of a serious case of theft or fraud being dealt with by the magistrates' court is therefore negligible. The loss of any automatic right to jury trial would be superfluous in cases such as these.

In any event the Government recognised that special considerations should apply in serous and complex fraud cases by instigating the Notice of Transfer system under SS4-6 Criminal Justice Act (1987). This procedure allows the Director of the Serious Fraud Office, the Director of Public Prosecutions,[5] the Commissioners of Inland Revenue, the Commissioners of Customs and Excise and the Secretary of State to give notice of transfer and thereby avoid the necessity of having the accused committed for trial.[6] The prosecution is therefore entitled by virtue of having given the notice to prefer a bill of indictment in respect of the relevant offences.[7] To protect the accused from trial on indictment where evidence is lacking the defence may apply to a Crown Court judge for a preparatory hearing in respect of the charges detailed in the notice of transfer with a view to dismissal of such charges and a quashing of the indictment.[8] The Royal Commission suggests (ibid., Ch. 7, para. 60) that this procedure be replaced by that which they recommend for all cases unless the rules can be amended to make them more amenable to serious or complex fraud cases. The recommended procedure is that preparatory hearings should become mandatory and part of the trial (ibid., Ch. 7, paras. 4, 5). The judge at such a hearing would be entitled to rule on questions relating to the admissibility of evidence and questions of law.[9] The only ground for appeal would be where the ruling was wholly unreasonable. (ibid., Ch. 7, para. 28). It is debatable whether this proposal would be more advantageous in serious or complex fraud cases[10] than that which already exists for preparatory hearings to take place under Sections 7 to 11 Criminal Justice Act 1987. These provisions were enacted following the recommendations of the Roskill Committee in 1986. Section 7 (1) of the Criminal Justice Act 1987 allows a Crown Court judge to order a preliminary hearing if the evidence "reveals a case of fraud of such seriousness and complexity that substantial benefits are likely to accrue from a hearing". Section 7 (1) (a) to (d) describe the purpose of the hearing as follows: (a) to identify the issues which are likely to be material to the verdict of the jury, (b) to assist their comprehension of these issues (c) to expedite the proceedings before the jury and (d) to assist the judge's management of the trial. Although the judge at a preparatory hearing may determine questions relating to the admissibility of evidence or points of law,[11] this has been restrictively interpreted[12] to refer to the purpose of the preparatory hearing under S7 (1) (a) to (d). Hence, the Royal Commission's proposed procedure would remove this restriction. The proposed procedure would also have the advantage of providing for preparatory hearings in all cases rather than the limited numbers of cases of the requisite gravity and complexity dealt with under the present procedure.[13]

There is no doubt as to the desirability of continuity in the hearing of fraud trials. The allocation of a judge to deal with a particular case *ab initio* should reduce the potential for delay and hence benefit the administration of justice. The Royal Commission clearly recognises the need for judges to be well-trained (ibid., Ch. 8, para. 77) and appears to implicitly accept the need for specialist judges.[14] However, the Royal Commission also suggests (ibid., Ch. 7, para. 31) that the trial judge should be bound by orders and rulings made by the judge at the preparatory hearing and counsel should be prohibited from seeking to re-open any matter decided at that hearing. This would seem to militate against trial continuity. Similarly, the recommendation that in a small number of cases the trial judge should be nominated as soon as the Crown Prosecution Service have alerted the court at a preparatory hearing that disclosure, severance or admissibility is sensitive and likely to be of critical significance, and, that the nominated judge should take over the management of the case right through to conclusion of trial, is unecessarily restrictive. It is submitted that nomination should occur at the outset.

The issue of delay and the necessity to shorten fraud trials has been uppermost in criticism of the present system.[15] The Royal Commission makes a number of recommendations designed to deal with these matters through procedural reform of both pre-trial and trial procedures generally. These include the imposition of time-limits in certain matters; for example, time limits should be imposed in pre-trial matters wherein the parties should certify that they have discussed the case and the result, and a "certificate of

49

readiness" given containing (*inter alia*) an estimate of the likely trial length. (ibid., Ch. 7, para. 22). As regards fraud trials it is suggested that targets should be set for the amount of time to be occupied by each stage of the fraud trial (ibid., Ch. 8, para. 80)[16] and where points of law have to be argued in the absence of a jury, written skeleton arguments should be submitted and time limits should be imposed on oral argument (ibid., Ch. 8, para. 80). This procedure already exists in civil cases and its introduction should be encouraged. Measures designed to encourage competence and efficiency by lawyers involved in trials generally are also included in the Royal Commission's report and appropriate sanctions suggested. The proposals would involved the Law Society and the Bar Council in the enforcement and promulgation of rules (ibid., Ch. 7, paras. 32-39) and empower judges to report barristers to the Professional Conduct committee of the Bar in specified circumstances (ibid., Ch. 7, paras. 32-33). Although the imposition of sanctions is given considerable emphasis by the Royal Commission it is submitted that this would necessitate the provision of considerable administrative support since judicial directions are often not complied with at present.[17]

The Royal Commission's proposals for increased defence disclosure have particular significance in the context of fraud trials.[18] These include the controversial suggestion that those who intend to contest charges should disclose their defence in advance of trial or indicate that they will not be calling evidence but will simply be arguing that the prosecution has failed to make out its case (ibid., Ch. 6, paras. 59, 62, 66, 67, 70-72). Subsequent failure to make out the defence or provision of contradictory explanation without good reason would entitle the prosecution, with leave of the judge, to invite the jury to draw adverse inferences and the circumstances should also be subject to judicial comment in the summing up (ibid., Ch. 6, para. 66). In principle, these suggestions would lead to early identification of the relevant issues thus limiting the evidence given at trial relating to agreed matters. However, the complexity of Serious Fraud Office investigations would mean an increase rather than reduce pre-trial delay since the defence would be obliged to deal with each point in issue to establish its defence at an earlier stage than it is at present required to do (ibid., Ch. 6, paras. 70-72). In cases involving co-defendants no interest could possibly be served by pre-trial admission of elements of the prosecution case.

Two key principles appear to be at stake as a result of the Royal Commission's proposals on disclosure.[19] The first relates to the burden of proof in criminal cases since this must be discharged in respect of the facts in issue in any particular case. The nature of the facts in issue will clearly be determined by referring to the legal ingredients of the offence and the defence which is raised. Pre-trial admission of facts by the defence necessarily means that the prosecution is not put to proof on these facts and there may be instances where the prosecution would not have successfully discharged their burden in respect of these admitted facts. The discrepancy between witness statements and oral testimony is likely to be accentuated in complex fraud cases. The second evidential issue implicit in the Royal Commission's proposals is concerned with the effect of advance disclosure requirements on the accused's now restricted right of silence the abolition of which was first proposed by the Home Secretary at the Conservative Party Conference on 7 October 1993. Although the authorities were difficult to reconcile, the basic principle that silence did not constitute an acknowledgement of guilt was well-founded.[20] It was also established that the accused's silence in response to an allegation could only amount to corroboration in limited circumstances.[21] Sections 34-39 Criminal Justice and Public Order Act 1994 made important restrictions on the right to silence. As regards pre-trial investigations S34 allows a court or jury to draw such inferences as appear proper from the evidence that the accused failed, on being questioned under caution or on being charged with the offence, to mention any fact relied on in his defence, being a fact which in the circumstances existing at the time he could reasonably have been expected to mention. Where S34 (1) applies a judge, in deciding whether to grant an application for dismissal of a charge of serious fraud under S6 Criminal Justice Act 1987 in respect of which notice of transfer has been given under S4 of that Act, may draw such inferences from the failure as appear proper. The section effectively aims to deter the defendant from raising a defence at his trial which was not disclosed to the police during interview. Section 35 deals with the accused's silence at trial providing that the court or jury may draw such inferences as appear proper from the accused's failure to give evidence or, having been sworn, refuses to answer any question without good cause. This section, according to Dennis (1995) does not establish whether there is a case to answer. Although these sections clearly increase the pressure on the accused to make early defence disclosure there is no duty to do so as would exist if the Royal Commission's proposals in this respect were fully implemented. An unsettled issue, if the Royal Commission's advance disclosure requirements were implemented, is the nature of the adverse inferences which the prosecution might invite the jury to draw, with the judges leave, should the defence fail to disclose the substance of their case or supply contradictory or mutually exclusive alternative defences where co-defendants are involved. It is submitted that any such proposal if implemented would further encroach unjustifiably on the accused's restricted right of silence since current principle does not permit it and its continued weakening or abolition on the grounds of expediency alone, bureaucratic political or administrative, is questionable.

The Royal Commission makes no proposals regarding the much debated issue of the abandonment of jury trials in serious fraud cases. It will be recalled that the Roskill Committee's report on fraud trials had recommended that in certain long and complex fraud cases either the prosecution or the defence might request the judge to order a trial by a special three man tribunal.[22] The proposed Fraud Trials Tribunal did not imply the demise of jury trial in complex fraud cases but its scope would have been limited by problems of interpretation caused by the recommended guidelines on what constituted "complexity" (Levi, 1986, p. 399). In any event, the proposal received scant support from practitioners[23] on the basis that there was no compelling evidence that juries failed to understand complex fraud cases any more than less complex cases and the number of "complex" cases was, notwithstanding, estimated as being extremely small in number. Lord Devlin echoed the view of many by pointing out that since the right of trial by jury was a constitutional convention cogent evidence should be required before its removal in such cases.[24] However, the recent dramatic collapse of the *Blue Arrow* and the second *Guinness* trials[25] and the length and cost of such trials has promoted a return to calls for an alternative system to jury trial in complex fraud cases.[26] The failure of the Royal Commission to follow or even adopt the Roskill Report recommendations on these issues is to be regretted since the time must surely have arrived for some kind of quasi-criminal procedure involving a full enquiry along the lines of the U.S. Securities and Exchange Commission regulatory system to be available in serious fraud cases.[27]

2   Sentencing

(a)   Criminal Justice Acts 1991 and 1993

The introduction of the "seriousness" criterion in S1 (2) (a) Criminal Justice Act 1991 and its subsequent amendment in August 1993 by S66 (1) Criminal Justice Act 1993 imposed a statutory framework applicable to all custodial sentencing. As Thomas has pointed out[28] (1993d, p. 12) S3 (3) effectively precludes the court from considering information other than that relating to the circumstances of the offence and associated offence(s) apart from that permissible under the revised S29 (1) which is concerned with the offender's previous convictions and the responses to previous sentences. However, S28 (1), which permits the court to take mitigating factors into account in fixing sentence, is relevant at the stage when the court is deciding whether to impose a custodial sentence under S1 (2) (a) and not simply to sentence length under S2 (2) (a).[29] Since the Criminal Justice Act 1991 provided no definition or guidance on when an offence was so serious that only a custodial sentence could be justified for the offence (S1 (2) (a)) or how the length of any custodial sentence could be made commensurate with the seriousness of the offence and associated offence(s) assessed under S1 (2) (a), (S2 (2) (a)) the courts have been forced to place increased reliance on guideline decisions of the Court of Appeal (Criminal Division) where they exist. In the case of theft by employees and professional persons in breach of trust the guideline case is *R v Barrick* (1985)[30]. In this case Lord Lane C.J. made the Court of Appeal's position clear by stating that:

> In general a term of immediate imprisonment is inevitable, save in very exceptional circumstances or where the amount of money involved is small. Despite the great punishment that offenders of this sort bring upon themselves, the Court should nevertheless pass a sufficiently substantial term of imprisonment to mark publicly the gravity of the offence.

In effect, the Court of Appeal was stating its view that thefts by employees and professional persons in breach of trust were in almost all cases so serious that only a custodial sentence could be justified and that view has been sustained in cases decided since the Criminal Justice Act 1991 came into force in October 1992, although, as Thomas points out, in each case substantial sums have been involved.[31] The Court of Appeal's reference in *Barrick* to publicly marking the gravity of the offence by sufficiently substantial terms of imprisonment appears contrary to the just deserts principles embodied in S1 (2) (a).[32] The Court in *R v Cunningham* (1992) recognised that prevalence was a matter relevant to the assessment of seriousness under S1 (2) (a) but emphasised that deterrence was a matter relevant to length of sentence under S2 (2) (a) and, in argument, an exemplary element in a sentence was not justified in applying S1 (2) (a). The matter could most effectively be dealt with by reducing or negating the mitigating factors taken into account under S28 (1). Clearly, the Act imposes an artificial restriction on the consideration of sentencing aims in theft and fraud cases and the assessment of seriousness which must be examined in the context of the circumstances of each case.

Section 5 (1) Criminal Justice Act 1991 amended S22 (2) Powers of Criminal Courts Act 1973 by substituting a new section which provided (*inter alia*) that the exercise by the court of the power to suspend a sentence could only be justified by the exceptional circumstances of the case. This has subsequently been restrictively interpreted by the Court of Appeal[33] and in two cases involving thefts by employees in breach of trust, *R v Lowery* (1992) and *R v Robinson* (1993), the court re-asserted the principle of immediate custody in *Barrick* and chose to ignore substantial mitigation. In *Lowery* the appellant had made two suicide attempts and expert evidence suggested he would be in need of continuing psychiatric care. Nevertheless Wright J. commented:

> This court has very much in mind the catastrophic effect that this man's dishonesty has had upon his career, his home and his whole life. Nevertheless, where, as here, a man who has been placed in a position of trust breaks that trust, he may frequently find himself visited with consequences which may go far beyond the immediate impact of any sentence that may be imposed upon him.

Similar sentiments were expressed in *Robinson* although there was no initial dishonesty, the appellant and her husband were bankrupt and he was hospitalised as a result of events. Although clearly part of a general policy towards reducing the availability of suspended sentences[34] which has great significance[35] these cases have also sought to stress the gravity of theft and fraud by employees and professional persons in breach of trust and therefore confirm the *Barrick* guidance.

(b)   The Court of Appeal (Criminal Division)

The relationship between fraud sentencing and the Court of Appeal's sentencing principles was explored by Levi in 1989. This involved an examination of how the *Barrick* guidelines were applied in practice (ibid., pp. 424-31). He concluded that the main dimensions of sentence variation in fraud cases were good/bad character, guilty plea/contested case, length of time over which the fraud was perpetrated and the amount of money involved. Although Levi acknowledges the conceptual difficulties of identifying the reasons for disparities he concludes that "there seem to be no principles that determine when the Court will decide whether or not circumstances are "quite individual" enough to justify departure from earlier cases". It is submitted that the conceptual difficulties Levi refers to are crucial in understanding the reasons for his inability to identify the principles used by the Court of Appeal in fraud cases with sufficient clarity. The work of Hogarth (1971) and Hood (1972) was crucial in identifying the human element as the major explanatory variable in sentencing decisions. Therefore, any analysis of legal principles or other factors commonly used by judges in specific cases such as fraud is bound to be inconclusive in explaining disparities since it fails to take into account the way in which information is selectively perceived by judges according to their attitudes and beliefs. Indeed, it is the penal philosophy of judges which emerged as the most important variable (Hogarth, 1971, Chs. 5, 18 and 21). Levi acknowledges this probability, without substantiation, by saying "... there are (probably unconscious) methods of smuggling in social prejudices as legitimate sentencing objectives" (Levi, 1989, p. 427). This criticism does not, of course, invalidate analysis of the emphasis given to certain mitigating or aggravating factors in fraud cases which is vital to jurisprudential development. My point is simply that this is not the same process as "explanation".[36] Levi's misconception is apparent in his second proposal for improving fraud guidelines; that "the **principles** of punishment used to justify different sentences for different offences or for the same offences at different times, would benefit from some disciplined treatment" (author's emphasis) (ibid., p. 431). The impact of public opinion on sentencers' perceptions of offending and their sentencing objectives is a subtle subjective psychological process (Hogarth, 1971, Ch. 18) and it is difficult to see how any "disciplined treatment" is either possible or desirable on the part of the executive or the judiciary.

We now turn to examine the treatment of certain aggravating and mitigating factors[37] by the Court of Appeal in recent cases of theft in breach of trust by employees and professional persons and fraud cases.

(i)   Aggravating factors

The Court of Appeal has continued to emphasise the degree of planning involved in fraud cases[38] as an aggravating factor but it is also the persistent nature of the activity which is significant. For example, in *R v Bingham* (1991) a typical case, the appellant was a partner in a firm of solicitors which specialised in trust administration. Approximately £730,000 was transferred by him to the accounts of several companies he controlled. The appellant had pleaded guilty to 11 counts of theft and one of procuring the execution of a valuable security by deception for which he received a total of six years' imprisonment. Hutchinson J. in the Court of Appeal declared "... having regard to what was a persistent and blatant misuse of client's money in breach of trust, and to the acute discomfiture and embarrassment of the firm and his partners we consider that the learned judge arrived at precisely the right sentence". This hardening of the Court of Appeal's attitude is evident in several recent cases[39] and represents a change from the more sympathetic approach displayed in earlier cases such as *R v Offord* (1985) where, as Levi points out (Levi, 1987, p. 267), in similar circumstances the sentence contained a mixture of retribution tempered by elements of personal mitigation, general deterrence and denunciation. In that case Watkins L.J. had commented "More moderate sentences than used to be passed are thought to be sufficient to assuage the sense of public outrage felt because of the kind of conduct which brings about serious abuses of trust."

The recent change in the Court of Appeal's approach to professional fraud has been prompted by a large number of mortgage fraud cases[40] in many instances involving very substantial sums. Sentencing guidelines for such cases were laid down recently in *R v Stevens and others* (1992) where the appellants had pleaded guilty to 37 counts which had taken place over a period of eight years, involving 128 mortgage applications for 90 different properties resulting in advances worth £1.8 million being obtained. Attempts were made in relation to a further £2.5 million with the lending institutions suffering an actual loss of approximately £250,000 some of which was covered by insurance.[41] In the Court of Appeal Leggatt L.J. emphasised that the role of the individual defendant was important in such cases and it was an aggravating feature if the offender recruited others to participate. He continued:

> Of relevance also is the length of involvement in the fraud
> or frauds by any particular defendant, as well as the
> extent of any personal benefit that he may have derived.
> It is of consequence, ..., whether there was a genuine
> intention to repay loans advanced, thereby ultimately
> avoiding loss to the financial institution concerned. It is
> common to pay regard to the amount obtained by the
> lenders, as well as to the losses suffered by them. ....It is
> important to bear in mind whether any particular
> defendant is a professional person or a quasi-professional
> person for the special reason that if such a participant he
> must necessarily be guilty of a breach of trust, and his

role may be an important one in the deception of the lending institution.

It is significant that the Court of Appeal concentrates on the nature of the breach of trust involved in theft by employees and fraud by professional persons although a distinction has been drawn between, for example, theft by postmen and thefts by employees in a business whilst professional persons can expect to be punished more severely.[42] It is clear from *Stevens and others* that in mortgage fraud cases the approach in *R v Evans* (1991) was too simplistic. There Morland J. stated "In our judgement by way of deterrence in most cases an immediate custodial sentence will be appropriate. Often, as in this case, an immediate custodial sentence will be appropriate". In *Stevens and others* Leggatt L.J. emphasised that there were many different kinds of mortgage fraud some of which were more sophisticated than others. It is essentially the defendant's role in the defrauding of the lending institution and his professional responsibility and capacity which are paramount.

(ii)   Mitigating factors

In 1989 Levi (p. 432) posed the question whether the secondary expected consequences of conviction should count as mitigation. In this Levi was referring to such things as the loss of job or career prospects which, he suggested, were viewed with differing impact by the Court of Appeal as between the professional fraudster and the ordinary petty criminal who may well be unemployed. In recent cases, such as *R v Mason* (1991) the Court of Appeal was firm in its view that loss of career prospects did not obviate the need to do justice as between offenders committing similar types of offence. However, an opposite opinion was expressed in *R v Devol* (1992) where, despite the fact that the facts involved a serious commercial fraud, Rougier J. stated "Particularly we bear in mind that in cases of this kind, the defendant suffers punishments and penalties other than those which can be imposed by the courts. This man has indeed lost everything that he had built up and, in these circumstances, we have come to the conclusion that perhaps a starting point of five years was somewhat too high." The Court of Appeal plainly takes a pragmatic approach to this issue. Nevertheless, the wider issue of whether process is punishment was given support by Leggatt L.J. in *Stevens and others* as was the impact of a guilty plea. The court emphasised that the nature and timing of the plea were significant as well as the character of the perpetrator and his age when he was a party to the fraud. This approach was also apparent in *R v Seal* (1989), *R v Weinberg* (1992) and *R v Bufffery* (1993). In the latter case Lord Taylor C.J. again stated the discretionary nature of the decision to apply a sentencing discount of about one-third for a guilty plea in fraud cases. The decision would be based on (*inter alia*) the timing of the plea and the strength of the case against the defendant. His Lordship was anxious to point out to fraudsters that they should not imagine that they would receive a substantial discount for a very late guilty plea. Nevertheless, the exercise of this particular aspect of judicial discretion may be in need of closer scrutiny following *R v Akbar* (1993) where one of the principal architects of the multi-million pound fraud which led to the collapse of the Bank of Credit and Commerce International (BCCI) in 1991 received a six year prison sentence. He had admitted 16 charges involving a total of approximately £500 million and could have expected a sentence of ten to eleven years' imprisonment. Mr Justice Scott Baker had indicated to the defendant that those who pleaded guilty in trials involving enormous expense "could expect a considerable discount in sentence."

(c)   The Royal Commission

The impact of a guilty plea on sentence received increased prominence following the recommendation of the Royal Commission on sentence discounts for guilty pleas (Royal Commission on Criminal Justice, 1993, Ch. 7, para. 47). The Commission suggested that this practice be formalised with earlier pleas attracting higher discounts.[43] The procedure would be initiated by the defendant and the "sentencing canvass" itself would take place in judges' chambers with both sides represented by counsel. The judge would indicate the maximum discount were the defendant to plead guilty at this stage and, if he did so, the case would move to open court (ibid., Ch. 7, para. 51). Although the procedure was suggested as a way of dealing with the "cracked trials" problem[44] it had substantive implications as did the parallel proposal that discussions on the level of charge (charge bargaining) should take place as early as possible to minimise the need for cases to be listed as conducted trials (ibid., Ch. 7, para. 56). In the event S48 Criminal Justice and Public Order Act 1994 was enacted which provides for sentence discounts by requiring the court to take into account the stage in the proceedings at which the offender indicated his intention to plead guilty and the circumstances in which this indication was given. If the court decides to discount the sentence in consequence it must state in open court that it has done so. As already indicated the issue of charge bargains and sentence discounts is particularly relevant to complex fraud cases where enormous expenditure in both time and money is incurred.

Tonry and Coffee have discussed some of the inherent conflicts in charge bargaining in the context of the United States. Their view is that such a process produces uncertainty in sentencing because the court may continue to sentence on the basis of the original or "real" offence (Tonry and Coffee in von Hirsch and Ashworth (eds), 1992). If institutionalised discounts or "charge reduction guidelines" were ever introduced it would penalise those who pleaded not guilty and discourage potential contested trials. It would also limit the amount of credit which the court may wish to give for a guilty plea. Finally, it would ensure that some specific discount would result from the guilty plea, whereas, as indicated, this does not necessarily occur in the absence of charge reduction guidelines. The alternative of "real-offence" sentencing whilst reducing the differential between sentences following pleas and those following trial produces illusory plea bargaining[45] and makes no allowance for a guilty plea. In the absence of institutionalised discounts the adoption of a sentence discounts procedure in recent legislation may, therefore, lead to an increase in "real-offence" sentencing and increase the influence of prosecutional discretion.

As Bottomley suggests "multiple charging is used to ensure a conviction on at least one charge, acting as a lever to a guilty plea" (Bottomley in Pease and Wasik, (eds) (1987). In complex fraud cases the pressures on the prosecution to accept pleas to the most serious readily provable offences which are consistent with the defendant's conduct may be intense. Certainly, if numerical guidelines were ever to be introduced in this country the prosecutor could charge a form of fraud which carried a much higher base-offence level than is consistent with the defendant's conduct. The risk for the defendant who does not plead guilty to the lesser charge is that if convicted of the more serious charge the judge cannot refuse the sentence under the guidelines.[46] There is no doubt, however, that such a system of guidelines would strengthen the prosecution and may lead to the evasion of the guidelines themselves through plea bargaining.[47]

3   Conclusion

The due process arguments against reform examined in this chapter have to be weighed against the undoubted time cost and inefficiency in the trial and sentencing of complex and serious fraud cases and the comparatively short sentences which result. As is so often the case public and political expediency have to be measured against what are considered to be

59

inalienable individual rights[48] and the principles[49] informing the criminal justice system[50] I would argue that the issues examined demonstrate an overwhelming need for urgent reform of the procedures for the trial and sentencing in serious fraud cases either by the adoption of the Fraud Trials Tribunal originally suggested by the Roskill Report or a quasi-criminal procedure with a full enquiry. Such extreme and urgent reform is not necessary in ordinary cases of theft by employees or professional persons in breach of trust. Although it has been argued that the proposals to reform criminal procedure made by the Royal Commission may have adverse consequences in such cases if implemented the Court of Appeal has recently responded constructively in developing guidance to deal with mortgage frauds. After numerous recommendations it is to be hoped that reform in serious and complex fraud cases is initiated without further delay.

References

1. The expression is used here to refer to theft by employees and professional persons in breach of trust and fraud cases.
2. *Practice Note (Model of Trial : Guidelines)* [1990].
3. New Sentencing Guidelines were issued by the Magistrates' Association in September 1993.
4. E.g. offence committed on bail, casting suspicion on others, committed over a period, large amount, planned, senior employee, sophisticated, vulnerable victim, previous convictions and failure to respond to previous sentences, if relevant.
5. Effectively this means the Crown Prosecution Service is empowered since the Director of Public Prosecutions is head of that organisation.
6. Although committals are replaced by new Transfer for Trial arrangements described in S44 and Schedule 4 Criminal Justice and Public Order Act 1994 these do not apply when a notice of transfer under S4 Criminal Justice Act 1987 has been served on the court; Schedule 4, para. 4 (2) (d). Crown Court fraud sentences are now subject to the Attorney-General's reference procedure; The Criminal Justice Act 1988 (Reviews of Sentencing) Order 1995.
7. S2 (2) (aa) Administration of Justice (Miscellaneous Provisions) Act 1933.
8. S6 Criminal Justice Act 1987.

9. In normal pre-trial reviews the only questions that may be determined relate to severance and/or amendment of the indictment.

10. Note that Schedule 9, paras. 29 and 30 Criminal Justice and Public Order Act 1994 substitute the words "seriousness or complexity" for "seriousness and complexity" in S4 (transfer of fraud cases) and S7 (preparatory hearings) Criminal Justice Act 1987.

11. S9 (3) Criminal Justice Act 1987.

12. *Re Gunawardena* (1990).

13. The Royal Commission also recommended the amendment of S10 (3) Criminal Justice Act 1987 to allow judges to put the issues before the jury at the outset of a long fraud trial (Ch. 8, para. 81). However, S10 (3) currently contains a restriction that no mention may be made to the jury of any information about the defence case disclosed at the preparatory hearing, subject to exceptions contained in S10 (1) and (2).

14. Apart from the current shortage of suitable judges this would have serious financial implications.

15. For summary and illustration of these issues see M Levi, (1984), (1991), (1993), p. 184.

16. This is clearly not supported by due process arguments. Similarly, Ch. 7, para. 23, would appear to give judges unfettered discretion; "the court should oversee the progress of cases and intervene to speed up the process if necessary."

17. See Ch. 7, para. 33. A code of practice for advocates is also suggested. See also comments by Glynn, (1993), p. 843.

18. For example, Ch. 7, para. 21. "Pre-trial procedures should be in practice directions and rules of court. Breaches should be subject to comment by the court, to costs sanctions and to disciplinary action."

19. Prior to the CJPOA 1994 defence obligations as to pre-trial disclosure of information was severely restricted. The general principal was that there was no obligation on the defence to disclosure the nature of their case except.

   (i) where, as discussed above, in a case of serious fraud the defence was ordered to supply a written statement indicating in general terms the nature of the defence; S9 (5) Criminal Justice Act 1987.

   (ii) alibi evidence - S11 Criminal Justice Act 1967.

   (iii) expert evidence - S84 Police and Criminal Evidence Act 1984.

20. *R v Mitchell* (1892).

21.   *R v Chandler* (1976). For discussion of the difficulties in applying the "even terms" doctrine see Murphy (1995), pp. 251-3. The right of silence in relation to the criminal investigation of fraud is discussed by Phippen, (1993), p. 17.

22.   Report of the Roskill Committee on Fraud Trials (1986) Ch. 8, para. 8. See also Zander (1986) and Levi (1986).

23.   See the dissenting opinion of Mr Walter Merricks.

24.   This argument has now attained wider significance in the light of the Royal Commission's proposals to abolish the automatic right to jury trial in either way cases.

25.   The Blue Arrow case lasted some 17 months from the beginning of the trial to the determination of the appeal at a cost to the taxpayer of between £35 million and £40 million.

26.   For example, Mr Justice Henry one of the judges in the second Guinness trial. The complexity and duration of the Maxwell cases makes a reassessment even more urgent.

27.   This idea is developed by Alastair Brett, *The Times*, 1 June 1993, p. 33.

28.   See also commentary on *Attorney General's Reference (No. 4 of 1993) (Bingham)* (1993).

29.   *R v Cox* (1993).

30.   The implications of this case in the context of fraud sentencing are discussed in Levi (1989), p. 424.

31.   See "Feature" Sentencing News, 3, 27 July 1993, p. 9 at p. 11.

32.   For discussion of the principles underlying the Act see Home Office, *Crime Justice and Protecting the Public* (1990).

33.   A process which began with *R v Okinikan* (1992).

34.   A trend which was reversed in *Cameron* (1993) (assault occasioning actual bodily harm) and *Huntley* (1993) (unlawful wounding). In the latter case provocation was accepted as "exceptional circumstances" although this had been rejected earlier in *Sanderson* (1992). In his commentary on *Bradley* (1994) Thomas suggests that such inconsistencies would be reflected in many first instance decisions leading to immediate imprisonment in cases where the "exceptional circumstances" would previously have resulted in suspended sentences. See *Campbell* (1995).

35.   Discussed by Thomas at (1993f), p. 722 and (1993g), p. 11.

36.   This does not deal with the continuing debate as to what constitutes an "explanation" in social science research.

37. Not all the factors mentioned in *Barrick* are considered, only those which have featured more prominently in recent cases.

38. See for example, *R v Michael* (1990) and *R v Munns* (1991).

39. For example *R v Griffiths* (1989) and *R v Wheeler* (1991).

40. For the financial implications of this see The Law Society, (1993).

41. A three year prison sentence was upheld on one appellant involved in 14 transactions and who had recruited or retained three others and twenty seven months for an appellant who took part in 20 transactions. A solicitor involved in only one transaction received a six month prison sentence and two years imprisonment was upheld for a mortgage broker who had been involved in 12 transactions.

42. See *R v Reid* (1992). However, a willingness to approve the principle of imposing a custodial sentence on evidently less serious cases of breach of trust is apparent in *R v McCormick* (1994).

43. The proposal was immediately criticised on the basis that it would pressurise defendants to wrongly admit offences, undermine the presumption of innocence and the necessity for the prosecution to prove its case. It was also suggested that it would unnecessarily penalise those who opted for jury trial and could operate to the disadvantage of ethnic minority offenders who tended to plead guilty more often. The Royal Commission recommended that the policy be kept under review to monitor its impact on ethnic minority communities.

44. This refers to those trials which abort at the last minute due to a change of plea. Eighty three per cent of defendants electing Crown Court trial change their plea to guilty.

45. Since the prosecution implicity promise the defendant a concession which is later diminished in value by the court or parole.

46. For a discussion of the problems produced by the 1987 Federal Sentencing Guidelines see Henham (1992), 21.

47. Schulhofer and Nagel (1990).

48. It has to be accepted that these rights which derive from the Classical School's desire for due process are historically not inalienable and change over time.

49. Perhaps we are now reaching the point where Blumberg's cynical view of the criminal justice process has become reality and due process is sacrificed in the name of bureaucratic and administrative expediency. See Blumberg, 1970, pp. 4-5.

50. Croall (1992) has summarised the main arguments concerning the relationship between punishment and white collar crime in the

criminal justice system. These arguments cause special difficulties. For instance, it is often assumed that some offenders are more deterrable than others. White collar offenders are assumed to fall into this category because as offences are assumed to be economically motivated they involve calculated risks by rational actors. Arguments that the "process is punishment" also reflect the potential deterrent value of the law since many offenders do in fact risk loosing their employment, reputation, high incomes, and comfortable lifestyles. Companies are also assumed to be future orientated, concerned about their reputations. Levi (1987) argued that unfavourable publicity and the experience of investigation, prosecution and trial can acts as deterrents in certain cases

Croall argues that the deterrent potential is undermined by the low rates of detection and prosecution and the limited impact of sentences. Just deserts creates a number of problems in relation to white-collar crime. According to Braithwaite and Pettit (1990) just deserts models rely on notions of guilt, blame and culpability, which could lead to less 'justice' for white collar offenders given their ability to minimise elements of intent and culpability. To prosecute all white collar offenders would also be prohibitively costly. Further, the principles of just deserts stress that punishment should reflect the harm done. However, Braithwaite and Pettit noted that offences are generally regarded as less serious and therefore any equation of punishment to harm done might be of little effect. Croall suggests that just deserts models may well perpetuate class based and ideological definitions of crime seriousness, therefore confirming the distinction between white-collar crimes and 'real crimes'.

Croall also suggests that other sentencing objectives have rarely been considered in the context of white collar crime, particularly corporate crime. High status white collar offenders are rarely seen as in need of help, advice and counselling, since they are assumed to have made rational choices whereas, in fact, some have suggested that rehabilitative policies may be *more* appropriate for this type of offender and the writer argues that incapacitation is a viable alternative for both individualised and corporate offenders - individual offenders are disbarred or disqualified; corporations are effectively incapacitated by closures or nationalisation.

Croall argues that since the impact of any sentencing policy may be limited more and more emphasis is placed on public protection and prevention, particularly effective self regulation which obviously requires the co-operation of companies.   Braithwaite (1984) suggests that effective regulation therefore requires both preventative policies and a range of different sentencing policies.

Croall cites Braithwaite (1989) as suggesting a viable alternative to the failed traditional approach of sentencing policy and crime control. This is the view that the most effective social control exists where offenders experience shame for their actions and where a wrongdoing attracts strong moral disapproval. The closest analogy to the 'family model of punishment' for white collar crime is self-regulation within organisations which would encourage moral disapproval of non-compliance. But this must be backed up by adequate levels of state punishment. Braithwaite argues that the problem with the adversarial approach is that it may make outcasts out of otherwise compliant businessmen and compliance strategies tend to underplay the moral educative function of the criminal law.

4   Violent Crime

1   Introduction

This chapter examines a number of problematic issues involved in the sentencing of violent offenders in England and compares the position in some European countries. It is argued that, unlike some of its European counterparts, the English system suffers from a lack of clarity in the definition of substantive offences and over reliance on judicially created sentencing principles which produces lack of coherence in the development of a sentencing policy for violent offenders. The argument is developed in the context of recent sentencing reform in England and other reform proposals.

Before embarking on a detailed examination of the English and European systems it is necessary to introduce a note of caution with regard to such comparative analyses. Writing in 1946 Stone drew attention to the difficulties inherent in developing a comparative jurisprudence (Stone, 1946, p. 48). He suggested a division between those kind of analyses which seek to develop a scheme into which the propositions of law of a particular country will fit ("particularist") and those analyses which seek to develop a logical scheme which is capable of application to all, or an indefinite class, of legal systems ("universalist").   Stone suggested that comparative jurisprudence lay somewhere between the two positions but should more particularly be regarded as "analytical jurisprudence applied in correlation to the propositions of several legal systems". Hence, comparative schemes were quite readily distinguishable from universalist schemes in the sense that it could not be assumed that what was common to two or more systems was applicable to all. The present discussion will clearly fall within the comparative rather than the universalist scheme making, as it does, comparisons and judgements between Roman and common law systems. In Stone's view such an exercise is noteworthy if only to lead to classification and simplification of the law but, essentially, he sees analytical jurisprudence as an exercise which would yield self-consistency in the body of legal propositions (Stone, 1946, pp. 51, 52). Stone also pointed out in later writings that there were recognizable limits on the effectiveness of proposed legal action (Stone, 1966, pp. 50, 51) and that proposals to extend the scope of an international legal order were subject to fundamental (and perhaps irreconcilable) questions about the nature of law and justice within state entities (Stone, 1966, p. 117). The more modest endeavour of "mutual helpfulness", as Stone puts it, should, however, remain a desirable and practical alternative and it is in this context that our discussion proceeds (Stone, 1966, p. 118).

It is proposed to examine certain concepts which are fundamental to penal policy formulation on the subject of sentencing violent offenders in Sweden, Finland, Italy, Greece and Germany and relate these to the English position. These comparisons are made to reflect European legal and cultural diversity and focus on offence definition, sentencing objectives, sentencing practices and the links which exist between substantive law and sentencing policy and practice.

2 The English Position

(i) The White Paper (1990)

The British Government's proposals for reform of the criminal justice system published in 1990 had important implications for the sentencing of violent offenders. The philosophical rationale of the resultant Criminal Justice Act (1991), its implications, and the subsequent case-law have all been the subject of extensive discussion in the appropriate literature and it is not proposed to rehearse such arguments here.[1] However, it is necessary to mention the key concept used in the reform proposals; that of "seriousness". This was used to refer either to seriousness in the offence, S1(2) (a), or the harm itself, S1(2) (b). Unfortunately, no definition of "seriousness" was provided and doubt was expressed as to how the provision stood in relation to the rule regarding the totality of sentences (Ashworth, 1991, p. 1). The problem was compounded by the fact that the same formula was repeated in SS2 and 6. Ashworth (1992) subsequently also suggested that the "dangerousness" provisions in the Criminal Justice Act (1991) posed certain difficulties (Ashworth, 1992b, pp. 163-167). For example, there could be cases which satisfied the protective provision in S1(2) (b) but not the seriousness provision in S1(2) (a). Further, the protective element added to the commensurate sentence had to be linked to the prediction of serious harm. Although S31(3) defined "serious harm" for this purpose nothing was said about determining the required degree of probability nor the assessment of serious harm. It therefore became necessary to consult White Paper (1990) which preceded the legislation to discover the Government's intentions (Ashworth, 1992a, p. 230).

The White Paper itself was at pains to point out that Government policy was based on the philosophy of just desert (see on this von Hirsch, 1976, 1986, and criticism by Galligan, 1981). It was explicitly stated that the severity of the sentence should be directly related to the seriousness of the offence (para. 1.6). Nevertheless, the principle was abandoned in the case of violent offenders posing a threat to public safety in favour of protective sentencing (para. 1.8). The main objective of sentencers was to express the principles of denunciation and retribution. As subsidiary aims a sentence could also be designed to protect the public, provide reparation or reform the offender (para. 2.9). Although none of these aims and their interrelationship were articulated in the legislation the theme running through the original proposals was unmistakably to expound the just desert philosophy in the context of the existing English retributivist sentencing system. Galligan (1981) had pointed out some ten years earlier that the emphasis on deserved sentences would make individualised sentences difficult to sustain, constrain sentencing discretion to the assessment of desert, and make the sentencer's task much more reactive than proactive (Galligan, 1981, pp. 300-301). Ashworth (1989) indicated that it was possible to achieve plurality in sentencing aims provided this was expounded in the legislation itself (as in Sweden) and guidance was given where aims conflict (Ashworth, 1989, p. 362). In the event, major operational difficulties caused the U.K. Government to abandon key elements in the Act. In May 1993 the Home Secretary announced the Government's decision to abolish the unit fine system as well as changing the Act's provisions on the assessment of seriousness and restrictions on the use of prior records (S1 (2) (a) and SS29 (1) and (2)).[2] This again raised important questions about the direction of penal policy and the need for consistency in sentencing offenders, particularly violent offenders. If the underlying aim of the Act was to reserve imprisonment for those who had committed serious offences such radical surgery to vital elements of the Act would threaten that objective. In summary, the apparent aim of the White

Paper to establish a rational sentencing policy for sentencing violent offenders failed to materialise.

(ii)   Substantive law issues

A lack of coherence in sentencing philosophy is mirrored in the English criminal law dealing with non-fal offences against the person. There are serious anomalies present in the definition of both the actus reus and mens rea elements and the penalties prescribed for the relevant offences created by the Offences against the Person Act (1861). Again, these problems have been well-documented and it is not proposed to re-consider them here.[3] It is important, however, to mention the various reform proposals. These were the subject of extensive and detailed debate in the Law Commission's Consultation Paper No. 122 (1992) which broadly adopted new offence definitions to reflect the relative seriousness of the offences originally proposed in the Draft Criminal Code Bill, Clauses 74-77, most of which in fact implemented the recommendations of the Criminal Law Revision Committee's 14th Report (para. 152). The reconstituted offences were, in the opinion of the Law Commission, consistent with the principle that the offender should be punished according to the type of injury that he intended or was aware that he might cause (para. 8.5). However, the Law Commission agreed with the Criminal Law Revision Committee's 14th Report, para. 154, that no attempt should be made to define "serious injury" since this was essentially a matter of judgement for the jury to decide.[4] Again, concurring with the Criminal Law Revision Committee, no attempt was made to define what was to be regarded as minor injury (falling within clause 6 of the Draft Bill), the Law Commission preferring instead the view that prosecutors would take the degree of injury into account when framing the charge and that, in any event, the extent of the injury would be a factor taken into account by a sentencing court in determining the possible penalty within the statutory maximum (para. 8.14). The actual definition of "injury" proposed in Clause 1(6) of the Draft Bill was extended as follows:- "injury" means:

(a)   physical injury, including pain, unconsciousness, or any other impairment of a person's physical condition, or

(b)   impairment of a person's mental health.

The Law Commission admitted that the law presently singled out those who contemplated violence as proper objects of deterrence and punishment on the basis of the harm they accidentally caused rather than because of the violence they contemplated and that this did not convey to the public that violence was taken seriously and that it would be punished according to the seriousness of the offender's conduct (para. 7.39). Further, the law should be governed by clear distinctions, expressed in modern and comprehensive language, between serious and less serious cases (para. 7.40). The idea that the actual culpability of the offender could be dealt with at the sentencing stage and that this could mitigate the apparent severity of some cases was rejected on the basis that intention and foresight are necessary determinants of liability in the first instance (para. 7.37). The writer would argue that if culpability is relevant for the legal definition of an offence to be satisfied then it must be satisfactorily dealt with in later stages of the process. The problem is that at the sentencing stage there has been no satisfactory policy or framework to deal with the concept whilst at the trial stage the concept has been distorted to comply with legal definitions. Furthermore, the two processes should be interdependent.

In the event the proposals described by the Law Commission in its Consultation Paper were largely adopted in its Report No. 218 (1993) which was accompanied by a Criminal Law Bill dealing with offences of violence. The proposed offences are detailed below and are designed to replace SS18, 20 and 47 of the 1861 Act:

2 (1)   A person is guilty of an offence if he intentionally causes serious injury to another (maximum sentence: life imprisonment).

3 (1)   A person is guilty of an offence if he recklessly causes serious injury to another (maximum sentence: five years' imprisonment).

4   A person is guilty of an offence if he intentionally or recklessly causes injury to another (maximum sentence: three years' imprisonment).

Clarkson (1994) has commented on the latest proposals and expressed a number of reservations:

(i)   In accordance with just desert theory he asserts that levels of criminal liability and punishment should generally be proportionate to the level of harm and degree of culpability with which the defendant acted. Clarkson suggests that those concerns are absent from the Law Commission's proposals on lesser injuries which fail to distinguish between intentional and reckless forms of the offence in terms of the appropriate punishment.

(ii)   There are doubts expressed as to whether the two categories of "injury" and "serious injury" are precise enough and the wisdom of leaving "serious injury" undefined for jury determination.

(iii)   The proposed definition of "injury" contained in clause 18 (identical to that proposed earlier in clause 1 (6) of the Draft Code Bill) is considered too broad. Clarkson takes the view that since the proposed new offence of causing injury is much more serious than assault it should be reserved for (relatively) more serious cases of injury with minor injuries only amounting to assault.

(iv)   Finally, the proposed definitions of intention and recklessness, in clauses 1 (a) and (b) respectively, are suspect in certain respects. Clarkson concentrates on the clear endorsement of subjectivism evident in clause 1 (b) which appears to assume a consensus which has been markedly absent in recent jurisprudential development of the meaning of "recklessness" in relation to common assault and S47 of the 1861 Act. He suggests that the substantive issue (as yet unresolved) is whether recklessness ought to be defined in subjective terms for the purposes of non-fatal offences against the person.

Clarkson is also critical of the Law Commission's proposals to retain certain special categories of assault and, particularly, clause 9 which extends the law relating to threats to kill to threats causing serious injury (maximum sentence: ten years' imprisonment). It is suggested that the maximum penalty is incongruous with that for an act actually causing serious injury where the maximum penalty is five years imprisonment. The substantive definition of assault in the Draft Criminal Law Bill is as follows:

6 (1)   A person is guilty of an assault if:

(a)   he intentionally or recklessly applies force to or causes an impact on the body of another -

(i)   without the consent of the other, or

(ii)   where the act is intended or likely to cause injury,   with or

71

without the consent of the other,
or

(b)   he intentionally or recklessly, without the
consent of the other causes the other to
believe that any such force or impact is
imminent.

(2)   No such offence is committed if the force or impact, not being intended or likely to cause injury, is in the circumstances such as is generally accepted in the ordinary conduct of daily life and the defendant does not know or believe that it is in fact unacceptable to the other person (maximum sentence: six months imprisonment).

The author agrees that the sentencing implications of the Law Commission's proposals to restructure non-fatal offences against the person continue to fail to distinguish sufficiently between different degrees of harm and blame (see Keating (1987 p. 570)). It is also difficult not to agree with Clarkson and Keating (1994, pp. 567-572, 813-815) that it is perhaps too restrictive to restructure these offences purely in terms of re-working combinations of mens rea and harm and that moral judgements should be incorporated in assessing relative seriousness, since culpability is a wider concept than mens rea.

Before turning to consider how other European countries have dealt with these issues it is important to emphasise the relevance of increased reliance on judicial discretion developed through Court of Appeal guidance, the Attorney-General's power to curb over-lenient sentencing and increased training provided by the Judicial Studies Board since the implementation of the Criminal Justice Act (1991). The significance of the Court of Appeal's role was highlighted by new parole provisions in the Act which did not provide any link between judicial sentencing and executive action thereby perpetuating the concept of executive sentencing. This matter was dealt with through the Practice Statement issued on 1 October 1992 to coincide with the implementation of the main body of the Act which in general terms broke with the traditional approach by requiring judges to decide questions of sentence with reference to parole. This was described by Thomas (1992) as undoubtedly the most significant judicial pronouncement on sentencing policy since the *Bibi* guidelines in 1980 (Thomas, 1992, p. 12).

3   Some European Alternatives

(i)   Sweden

In Sweden new provisions covering the determination of sanctions i.e. choice of sanction and determination of punishment were introduced into the Penal Code's provisions on 1 January 1989 with the aim being to increase the predictability and consistency of penal decision-making (Lundquist, 1990, p. 103). The punishment is determined by the penal value attributed to the offence which requires special consideration to be given to the harm, wrong or danger occasioned by the criminal act, what the offender realised or ought to have realised about it, as well as his intentions or motives (Chapter 29, p.1). A number of aggravating circumstances in the assessment of penal value are provided, for example, whether the offender exploited some other person's vulnerable position or special difficulties in protecting himself. Special consideration must also be given to a number of mitigating circumstances in assessing penal value. Guidance is also given on the impact of previous criminality and factors over and above the penal value of the crime to which the court may give reasonable consideration e.g. whether the offender has suffered serious bodily harm as a result of the crime. Imprisonment is used where the penal value of the offence is high and when the offender's previous record is such that it precludes consideration of any other sentence. The definition of assault in the Swedish Penal Code differs substantially from the English equivalent. Chapter 3, Section 5 of the Code defines assault as inflicting bodily injury, illness or pain upon another or render(ing) him unconscious or otherwise similarly helpless. Chapter 3, Section 6 of the Code states that if the assault is considered grave the sentence will be for aggravated assault, and, in judging the gravity of the crime, special attention shall be paid to whether the deed involved a mortal danger or whether the offender had inflicted grievous bodily injury or severe illness or had otherwise shown great ruthlessness or brutality.

In their comparative study of violent crime in Scotland and Sweden, McClintock and Wikstrom (1990) noted that problems of comparability might be produced by differences in demarcation between serious and petty assault and that they were best combined with attempted homicides and treated as a single category (McClintock and Wikstrom, 1990, pp. 211-212). Although the category of aggravated assault should contain specified ingredients many phrases remain undefined. Guidance is now provided on the aggravating circumstances to be taken into account in assessing penal value. This does not exist in English law where, according to S3 (3) (a)

Criminal Justice Act (1991), the court may take into account all such information about the circumstances of the offence (including any aggravating or mitigating factors) as is available to it. The actual aggravating factors which might be permitted are not elucidated. Personal mitigation is irrelevant at this stage but S28 (1) provides that nothing shall prevent a court from mitigating an offender's sentence by taking into account any such matters as, in the opinion of the court, are relevant in mitigation of sentence. Furthermore, as we have seen, the Draft Criminal Law Bill does not distinguish between injury and serious injury nor the manner in which the harm is inflicted.

According to Lundquist (1990) it is probably too early to say whether the Swedish review has led to any reduction in the use of imprisonment in the long term thus reversing a trend in the direction of more severe penalties evident during the 1970s and 1980s. As he points out, the committee which made provision for the determination of sanctions found that existing penal value assessment failed to conform to perceived societal norms and recommended rises in penal values for crimes of violence. This was reflected in a corresponding decrease in penal values for property offences. A similar result was achieved through the adoption of the "seriousness criterion" in the English Criminal Justice Act (1991) with corresponding re-focusing of community sentences as punishment in the community. Arguments concerning the success of such strategies in achieving reductions in the prison population are beyond the scope of this analysis. The important differences between the two countries which have a direct bearing on the sentencing of violent offenders relate to the Swedish articulation of the procedure for penal value assessment and its relevance to clearly defined offence definitions. This is lacking in English sentencing policy.

(ii)   Finland
In 1977 the Penal Law Committee in Finland set out three principles that would be applied to all forms of punishments. It stated that the punishments:
- should not be cruel
- should reflect the principles of proportionality and equality
- should be directed at the offender alone
- should not cause needless suffering
- should not cause unregulated culmination of sanctions; and
- should be economical from the point of view of society.

The Penal Law Committee proposed the abolition of indeterminate sanctions in Finland in 1977. In 1971 the law had been amended to permit indeterminate sentences only in the case of violent offenders who had committed a crime of violence resulting in a sentence of at least two years' imprisonment and who had in the ten years prior to the offence been guilty of another offence involving aggravated violence or special damages to the life or health of another. The present Finnish sentencing provisions are contained in Chapter 6 of the Penal Code which combines general principles with specific sentencing criteria. These principles are similar to those of Sweden and, again, the guiding principle is that of just desert (Lappi-Seppala, 1990).

> In sentencing, all the grounds increasing and decreasing the punishment that affect the matter and the uniformity of sentencing shall be taken into account. The punishment shall be measured so that it is in just proportion to the harm and risk involved in the offence and to the culpability of the offender manifested in the offence (Finnish Penal Code 6, p. 1).

Chapter 6 of the Code also contains the principles of sentencing according to the notion of normal punishments which consists of two elements. Points of similarity with what may be described as a typical offence of the instant case are noted and the appropriate punishment is selected. Hence, the concepts of the "normal offence" and "normal punishment zone" are included in the Finnish Penal Code. Statistical data provide the information which describes the effect of certain sentencing criteria and different manifestations of the typical offence. Such analyses have been produced in the case of assault (*inter alia*). The analyses allow the courts to evaluate what penalties have been imposed for offences committed in approximately the same manner, where the harm inflicted is similar and where the offenders have broadly similar criminal records. As Lappi-Sappala (1990) indicates, however, "Legal theoretical analysis and the decisions of higher courts are intended, *inter alia*, to develop more specific sentencing criteria and to make reasoned suggestions about their meaning in different situations"; a role increasingly attributable to the English Court of Appeal. Finnish judges are still therefore called upon to exercise their discretion in the interpretation of higher court decisions and sentencing criteria.

In common with similar systems the Finnish sentencing system endeavours to ensure sentencing consistency by ensuring that the scale of crimes and punishments are related to each other in the actual decision-making process. The success of such a strategy depends on reaching agreement about the relevant criteria. The relative scaling of offences and punishments must ultimately remain arbitrary and carries with it the risk that it may fail to correspond with public perceptions of seriousness and just desert. Nevertheless, Lappi-Seppala (1990, p. 131) argues that existing sanction levels have not been consolidated with the adoption of the zones of normal punishments model in the case of drunken driving and theft offences. In cases of drunken driving the provisions were aimed at reducing the use of unconditional prison sentences and with theft cases the aim had been to effect a reduction in the use of disproportionate sanctions when compared to other offences. Both objectives appear to have been achieved. There is no reason to suppose that sentencing criteria could not be devised to establish the equivalent of a zone of normal punishments in the English context. The main difficulty would lie in producing statistical data relevant to the concept of the "normal offence" in cases of violence against the person since the information itself would merely reflect inadequacies in the legal classification of such offences as they currently exist.

(iii)   Italy

The Italian Penal Code, Article 70 details the objective circumstances surrounding the commission of an offence such as aspects of the act itself, seriousness of the injury or peril caused by the crime, and personal conditions or characteristics of the victim, and, subjective circumstances, such as degree of fault, relationship between the accused and the victim. Article 61 defines examples of common aggravating circumstances such as contemptible or trifling motives for the crime, the use of torture or cruelty, the aggravation or attempt to aggravate the consequences of crime. Common attenuating circumstances are defined in Article 62 e.g. motivation through moral or social values, provocation. Attenuating and aggravating circumstances apply irrespective of the knowledge of the accused and are applied objectively. Where similar attenuating or aggravating circumstances exist a decrease in penalty proportional to the number of circumstances considered may be made by the court, whose decision is not subject to review; Article 63. Detailed provisions exist to deal with the influence of aggravating circumstances or punishments; Articles 63-69.

Italian law recognises different categories of assault ranging from Article 581, where the act of striking another does not result in physical or mental illness to Article 582, personal injury, where someone causes personal injury to another resulting in physical or mental illness. Aggravating circumstances are dealt with in Article 583. This Article also describes those circumstance which may result in the injury being classed as serious or very serious and thus meriting a longer term of imprisonment. For example, personal injury is serious if it produces permanent impairment of a sense or organ and very serious if it produces loss of a sense, limb, mutilation rendering the limb useless, loss of use of an organ or ability to procreate, permanent and serious speech impediment, or deformity or permanent disfigurement of the face. An offence of negligent personal injury is created by Article 590 with increasing penalties depending on the seriousness of the offence.

The significance of the Italian system for present purposes lies in the fact that both the criminal law and the principles of punishment are creatures of legislation. No factual situation can constitute a criminal offence unless it has been classified as such at the time the act occurred and similarly all penalties are expressly defined by legislation. There is, therefore, no tradition of judicial interpretation of either the criminal law or criminal sanctions. Although the principle clearly accords with the Classical tradition of preventing the arbitrary abuse of power it is alien to the common law traditions of extensive interpretation and sentencing by analogy. The re-defined offences in the Draft Criminal Law Bill in England are much less precise than their Italian counterparts and only inflexible sentencing guidelines promulgated by Parliamentary legislation would approximate the rigidity of the Italian system. Therefore, although the result may be desirable in providing an integrated sentencing policy for dealing with violent offenders it cannot be transposed to the English context.

(iv)   Greece

The Greek Penal Code shares many of the characteristics of its Italian counterpart in its Classical origins but has also been historically influenced by both the German and Swiss Penal Codes. One of the most important principles deduced from the Code, Article 1, is that no penalty may be imposed on the basis of a penal law not describing specifically the criminal behaviour and not providing the applicable penal sanctions within upper and lower limits. However, mitigation of criminal liability is achieved either through custom, inference by analogy or retroactive recent laws. The objectives of Greek penal law have been stated as being:

(a)   individual or special prevention through reform or re-education, fear of punishment and incapacitation, and,

(b)   general prevention especially through "moral propaganda" teaching obedience to law and strengthening the norms but also through fear of punishment. (Bishop, 1988, p.227).

The Greek Penal Code (Chapter 16) details a considerable number of offences classed as Bodily Injury viz. Article 308, Simple Bodily Injury; Article 309, Grievous Bodily Injury; Article 310, Severe Bodily Injury; Article 311, Deadly Injury (i.e. bodily injury causing death); Article 312, Bodily Injury of Minors; Article 313, Brawling; Article 314, Negligent Bodily Injury. Guidance is given as to the meaning of severe illness to the mind or body of the victim which constitutes the offence of Severe Bodily Injury under Article 310 i.e. it exists if as a result of the offence the victim is in danger of his life or contracts a severe and lengthy illness or is seriously mutilated or in any way prevented from using his mind or body for a long period of time and to a serious extent.

The Penal Code also details several articles dealing with how the court should fix a sentence within the parameters identified by the Code. Article 79 of the Penal Code (Judicial Computation of Punishment) provides that the court when fixing sentence must in determining the nature of the offence consider:

(a)   the injury resulting or the danger presented

(b)   the quality, type and purpose of the offence as well as circumstances attending its preparation or commission, and

(c)   the extent of intent or degree of negligence of the offender.

The court must also give reasons justifying the imposed punishment. These are particularly important and their absence may theoretically result in a successful appeal to the Supreme Court. However, in practice the Supreme Court has held that general reference to the appropriate legal terminology is sufficient without any specific reference to particular circumstances. Again, in similarity with the Italian system, the Greek provisions do not attempt to detail specific guidance on degrees of seriousness within offence categories which can be directly related to sentencing provisions. Calculation of punishment is confined to issues which are dealt with in England in the context of the Court of Appeal's sentencing principles (Thomas, 1979, Ch. 2). Nevertheless, one important goal of Greek criminal policy during recent years has a direct bearing on sentencing violent offenders. This is to expand the alternatives to prison in common with most Western European countries. Non-custodial penalties are not expressly provided by the Greek Penal Code although a number of unrelated alternatives are mentioned. Hence, for less serious offences (petty violations) resulting in custody, Article 82 provides that all custodial sentences not exceeding six months will as a rule be converted into pecuniary penalties. The court must give specific reasons for its decision and must take into account the financial circumstances of the offender when setting the specific pecuniary penalty. However, non-custodial sanctions are not available for felonies and most misdemeanours, but, if the imposed sentence for any offence i.e. the sentence fixed following mitigation, does not exceed 18 months' imprisonment conversion is then possible. Such a policy provides limited flexibility in an otherwise rigid sentencing system and it should also be seen against the background of a two-thirds parole eligibility date; Articles 105-110. It still fails to provide any rationality in the sentencing policy for violent offenders as a whole and affects only a small number of cases.

(v)   Germany
The German Penal Code (GFR), Section 17, distinguishes a number of offences according to their relative seriousness viz. para. 223, Bodily Harm; para. 223a, Dangerous Bodily Harm; para. 224, Aggravated Bodily Harm; para. 225, Intentional Aggravated Bodily Harm; para. 230, Negligent Bodily Harm. It is interesting to note that dangerous bodily harm involves the use of a weapon, or sneak attack, or action by several persons acting in concert, or by life endangering act. The possible use of a weapon is also contemplated by the English offence of malicious wounding and inflicting grievous bodily harm under S20, Offences against the Person Act (1861) although no guidance is provided as to what constitutes grievous bodily harm. Para. 224 of the Penal Code states that aggravated assault is committed if the victim suffers loss of an important part of his body, sight in one or both eyes, hearing, speech or his procreative capacity, or the assault results in a serious permanent deformity or deteriorates into invalidity, paralysis or mental illness.

Judicial sentencing is circumscribed by legislative scaling of penalties which provides for cases which differ in gravity from the average type of offence and do not fit within the normal levels provided. In such cases judges may evaluate aggravating or mitigating circumstances according to guideline examples or exercise complete discretion if necessary. As Huber (1982, p. 21) argues:

this statute therefore ensures through careful gradation of the different forms of commission of the offence that a certain uniformity is achieved in sentencing and, at the same time, that the judge retains his discretion to consider the actual case under trial with regard to individuality of the act and the actor.

There is still, however, considerable scope for judicial discretion in fixing the actual prescribed sanction with the upper and lower limits although the Penal Code provides explicit principles for the determination of punishment in para. 46. Apart from stating in para. 46 (1) that the foundation of punishment is guilt and that the judge must consider the effects of the punishment on the offender's future life, many factors circumscribe how the nature and extent of any penalty is decided with reference to the purpose of punishment in the individual case. The principles of punishment in para. 46 state that all the circumstances, both mitigating and aggravating, must be taken into account by examining certain listed factors. For example, the motives and aims of the offender, the manner of perpetration and the wrongfully caused effects of the act, the offender's conduct after the crime are cited as relevant. It is significant that para. 46 (3) specifically states that circumstances which already represent the statutory constituent elements of the crime may not be taken into account. Mitigation rules are presented by para. 49 which provide margins replacing through mitigation the sanction originally imposed. Heinz (1989) describes how two new sanctions of dispensation with punishment and cautioning with deferred sentence were introduced in the 1969 reforms as well as measures affecting the use of imprisonment, fines, probation and parole. He concludes that the reforms to the Penal Code were not immediately accepted and implemented by the courts and the criminal law reform appears to strengthen polarisation between substantive law and sentencing practice. This was disappointing in view of the fact that the object of the reform was stated to be to use the sentencing system as "an appropriate instrument of criminal policy for the prevention of future offences, particularly by rehabilitation of the offender." Graham (1990, p. 167) also concludes that the West German experience illustrates that it is perhaps unwise to abandon efforts to divert offenders from custody in favour of efforts to influence sentencers to reduce sentence lengths. It may be that the crucial issue is the number of receptions into prison rather than sentence lengths. If this is correct it is not surprising that recent English reforms did not guarantee success in reducing the prison population. There were no offence reforms and great reliance was placed on the development of judicially created sentencing principles, White Paper (1990, p. 5), para. 2.3).

4   Conclusions

It has been argued that there are weaknesses in the present English system of sentencing violent offenders which require urgent attention. These weaknesses may be summarised as follows:

1)   No specific sentencing policy for violent offenders based upon agreed aims or objectives exists. The seriousness criterion based on just desert described in the White Paper (1990) and enumerated in the Criminal Justice Act (1991) applies to all offence categories. It is not made clear how the just desert aim is achieved in individual cases by balancing the harm and dealing with the culpability of the offender in violent offence cases.

2)   No rational and clear statement in substantive law of violent offence categories exists. The present law is highly anomalous and does not distinguish sufficiently between different degrees of violence or harm. The Law Commission's recent proposals do not take this issue significantly further.

3)   No useful link between substantive law and sentencing policy exists. This is necessary in order that uniformity is achieved between the different forms in which the offence may be committed and the punishment selected in individual cases.

4)   Undue reliance is placed on judicial sentencing policy and subjective assessment. This is a deliberate strategy (c.f. White Paper (1990)) which leaves the crucial issue of consistency in sentencing violent offenders firmly in judicial hands for the foreseeable future.

The Scandinavian experience shows that it is possible to attempt the vital link between substantive criminal law and sentencing practice by specifying in what circumstances punishment may be applicable according to the penal value of the crime. It is clearly necessary to articulate the criteria involved with great precision. However, as we have seen, English offence categories are not amenable to any such link. Even the re-designed offences proposed by the Draft Criminal Law Bill place great reliance on distinguishing offences in terms of the mental element required when it is the different degrees of harm which need to be more closely defined.[5] Any re-designed offences should deal with factors such as the degree of harm, degree of violence, and mental attitude of the offender. Such factors could be linked directly to specific sentencing guidelines to allow for the calculation of penal value for the offence. These would be detailed and include criminal history, mitigating circumstances and aggravating circumstances as well as those factors referred to in the definitions of the offences.[6] Alternatively, it is submitted that there is a case within the context of the attempts to strengthen the Court of Appeal's role in providing guideline judgements, to create one offence of violence against the person punishable with a maximum sentence of, say, 14 years' imprisonment in the Crown Court and six months' imprisonment in the magistrates' courts. It would then be open to the Court of Appeal to oversee the exercise of sentencers' discretion and develop guidelines dealing more specifically with vital issues such as the degree of harm and the degree of violence offered. The alternative to this is clearly some form of sentencing guidelines, an idea which has been rejected by the U.K. Government. A compromise solution might be to adopt a firm policy by concentrating on definite seriousness indicators within existing offence categories such as those suggested in The Magistrates' Association Sentencing Guidelines, 1993[7]. However, none of this would remove the anomalies inherent within the existing legal categorisations of these offences.

It is perhaps appropriate to conclude with some comments on the relevance of "justice" to the debate about the sentencing of violent offenders. Stone (1979) has emphasised the point that jurisprudential concepts such as "fairness" and "equality" should not be equated with justice since there is no empirical justification for such an assertion (Stone, 1979, p. 114). Indeed, he tries to demonstrate that, empirically at least, justice may require not equality but rather differentiation in distribution or treatment. This is relevant to the fundamental dilemma of balancing a sentencing system founded on desert theory against the need to achieve justice or a just solution in any particular case. Unless sentencers are forced to rationalise their decisions in terms of achieving just desert then it will always be arguable that the sentence is justifiable with reference to some other penal aim(s) and, ultimately, that it represents an individualised sentence where numerous factors were given due consideration and a just solution emerged. This is particularly important when assessing the degree of violence and its impact on the victim. It is arguable that desert theory is not necessarily commensurate with justice since the latter concept is not susceptible to any kind of objective definition. However, as Matza (1964) has indicated, "the major dimensions of justice are known to most members of society in a crude and intuitive way because justice is a crucial aspect of the common sense of modern democratic nations" (Matza, 1964, p. 105). Matza, therefore, does feel able to equate justice with fairness since ultimately it becomes a moral question of deciding which values should inform the sentencing system. It is important that we do not lose sight of the fact that the values which society wishes upheld should be those which inform any reform of the sentencing system. As Ashworth (1989) points out "Sentencing is the stage after the imposition of criminal liability and may be characterised as a public, judicial judgement of the degree to which the offender may rightly be ordered to suffer legal punishment" (Ashworth, 1989, p. 340). By concentrating on the mechanics of proportionality and desert it is easy to overlook these vital issues which do not appear to have been given sufficient prominence in the U.K. Government's deliberations. These matters are important simply because it is moral judgements as much as any factor which will dictate the sentencer's approach to dealing with those offenders convicted of violent offences.

References

1. See, for example, Wasik and von Hirsch (1990), Ashworth (1992b), Criminal Law Review (April, 1992), Thomas (1993).

2. Accomplished by Section 65 and Schedule 3 (fines) and Section 66 (previous convictions) Criminal Justice Act (1993).

3. For discussion of these issues see, for example, Keating (1987), Smith (1992), Clarkson and Keating (1994).

4. For criticism of these proposals see, Williams (1990).

5. This accords with the broader approach proposed by Clarkson and Keating (1994, p. 809 et seq).

6. Note Galligan's warning that the guidelines approach is only a technique for distributing penalties and does not seriously consider the policies behind them or the methods used to achieve them; (1981, p. 309).

7. For a discussion of the "seriousness" issue in the context of the 1992 guidelines see Wasik and Turner (1993, p. 352).

5　Dangerous Offenders

1　Introduction

This chapter analyses Court of Appeal guidance on the use of the protective sentencing provisions contained in the Criminal Justice Act 1991. It is argued that the Act's desert principles have proved an illogical and inadequate basis for justifying protective sentences. The chapter examines the genesis of the provisions in the 1990 White Paper, recent case-law concerning the scope of the provisions and concentrates particularly on developing the argument through an analysis of the Court of Appeal's approach to the determination of dangerousness within the parameters set by the legislation. This discussion pays particular attention to the balance required between the assessment of risk and harm and their inter-relationship. The inconsistencies revealed are further explored by considering the provisions determining the length of protective sentences including the impact of sentence discounts and the deficiencies in parole provision. The chapter continues with an examination of possible alternative strategies and procedures and finally concludes that the future interpretation of the protective provisions represents a major challenge to the Court of Appeal in the future development of sentencing policy.

2　Background

The introduction of protective sentencing provisions in the Criminal Justice Act 1991 were justified in the 1990 White Paper[1] which preceded it in terms of general desert principles. In para. 1.8 it was stated:

The police give priority to detecting the most serious crimes, since the public needs protection from those who commit them. Long prison sentences are the right punishment for these offences.

And again in para. 2.2:

Punishment in proportion to the seriousness of the crime has long been accepted as one of the many objectives in sentencing. It should be the principal focus for sentencing decisions. This is consistent with the Government's view that those who commit very serious crimes particularly crimes of violence should receive long custodial sentences.

Nevertheless, in para. 3.13 it was made clear that the forthcoming provisions were to be regarded as an exception to desert proportionality principles;

The Government proposes to take this approach further by giving the Crown Court[2] power to give custodial sentences longer than would be justified by the seriousness of the offence to persistent violent and sexual offenders, if this is necessary to protect the public from serious harm. There are a small number of offenders who become progressively more dangerous and who are a *real* risk to public safety... The proposed restrictions on the use of custody will not apply to the most serious crimes which are tried only in the Crown Court. Some offenders will be convicted of less serious offences but the Crown Court will recognise that they are a *serious* risk to the public. In these circumstances, the Government considers that an exception should be made to the principle that the length of the individual sentence should be justified by the seriousness of the offence (emphasis added).

Hence, selective incapacitation was introduced in the Criminal Justice Act 1991[3] yet its philosophical rationale was not made explicit. Nowhere is this lack of clarity greater than in para. 2.9 of the 1990 White Paper:

The Government's proposals therefore emphasise the objectives which sentencing is most likely to meet successfully in whole or in part. The first objective for all sentences is denunciation and retribution for the crime. Depending on the offence and the offender, the sentence may also aim to achieve public protection, reparation and reform of the offender, preferably in the community. This approach points to sentencing policies which are more firmly based on the seriousness of the offence, and just deserts (*sic*) for the offender.

This para. appears to imply that such forward-looking objectives as public protection, reparation and reform of the offender are somehow logically justifiable secondary outcomes of measures based principally on a just deserts approach. However, in reality such objectives can be considered utilitarian by-products of just deserts rather than justified by it.[4] For example, in the case of the relevance of past convictions, it could be argued that these should increase deserts whilst at the same time it may be suggested that they justify the imposition of a deterrent sentence. The 1990 White Paper made it appear that just deserts was capable of justifying a wide variety of sentencing outcomes when this was clearly not the case.[5] Notwithstanding this apparent confusion regarding desert implications, the protective sentencing provisions contained in the 1991 Act were described as an exception to just deserts principles. This departure from the proportionality principle had been subject to consistent and severe academic and popular criticism prior to the Act's implementation.[6] The main thrust of the criticism was that the notion of selective predictive confinement for persistent serious violent and sexual offenders was morally unjustifiable. Such offenders could be adequately dealt with under the (then) existing system[7] and since predictive techniques were largely inaccurate[8] selective incapacitation on dangerousness ground was unsustainable. It was nevertheless argued by some[9] that such moral arguments were subject to utilitarian advantages of social benefit in the form of limited crime prevention.[10] Ultimately, the debate is concerned with the identification of those rights which the criminal justice system should protect. A penal policy which sustains a right to individual liberty would maintain that this principle should not be sacrificed in the interests of crime control. Logically, this may result in the case of so-called dangerous offenders in a missed opportunity to prevent further lawbreaking if we accept that the level of probability that further lawbreaking will take place is morally unacceptable. As Ashworth points out (Ashworth, 1979, p. 418) however, the corollary of accepting the individual rights position is that the failure to incarcerate the guilty may impact on the individual rights of future victims. He goes on to state:

> In order to decide whether in a particular type of case it is justifiable to curtail or even to take away a right, it will therefore be necessary to assess the relative importance of the right, to evaluate the social benefits which are claimed to result from its curtailment, and then to decide whether the expected increase in crime control is worth the sacrifice of the right... the sustantive issues of evaluation remain to be resolved. For that, nothing more than conscientious and principled argument can be prescribed.

The argument in the case of protective sentencing was resolved in favour of the potential victim although the issue remain controversial.[11] However, the legislation itself went further in its encroachment on individual rights than originally anticipated. This was hinted at in para. 3.13 of the 1990 White Paper[12] and made explicit by the Home Office Minister, Mr John Patten;

> We need to consider carefully whether we can rely on offenders from whom the public needs to be protected always having previous convictions of a similar nature. This may be exceptional to rare, but there may be offenders whom the courts judge, from their pattern of behaviour to be dangerous but who have never been convicted before.... The protection of the public is so important that it would not be right to let the court's ability to afford the public this protection to hang on whether the offender had previous convictions.[13]

Both the wording of S1 (2) (a) and (b) which appeared in the original Bill and the Act which received the Royal Assent made it clear that para.s (a) and (b) were to be regarded as alternative grounds for imposing custody. It is evident that para. (b) does not require the offender to have been convicted of an offence which is so serious that only a custodial sentence can be justified for it. Indeed, as Wasik remarks, to interpret the provision otherwise would render para. (b) superfluous to para. (a) which would cover all cases (Wasik, 1993, p. 131). It is therefore possible for a protective sentence to be passed under para. (b) where the offender is convicted of a relatively non-serious offence on the present occasion. This certainly increases the potential availability of the sentence in the magistrates' courts although its effectiveness in terms of public protection is severely curtailed by the maximum sentences available for the relevant offences. Ashworth had speculated (Ashworth, 1992b, Ch. 6, pp. 163-167) as to the kind of case which could have represented the lowest threshold for S1 (2) (b) and the pre-Act indecent assault example in *R v McFarlane* (1989) does in fact correspond with the post-Act case of *R v Bowler* (1993) which confirmed that it is unnecessary to establish that the defendant has caused serious harm in the past in order to form the opinion that there was a danger that serious harm might occur in the future. The increased potential for encroachment on individual rights confirmed by *Bowler* relates to the predictive issue. Both actuarial and clinical methods of determining dangerousness rely heavily on past record. Actuarial methods depend on assigning an individual to a risk group based on measurable factors such as sex, age and criminal record[14] whereas most clinical methods have been based on predictive studies that have examined offenders mainly convicted of violent sex offences.[15] Given the notorious unreliability of such predictive techniques[16] it may be argued that prediction of future behaviour unsupported by evidence relating to past behaviour further weakens the likely accuracy of the prediction becoming reality.[17] Against this, however, it is always possible to argue that an acceptable balance has to be maintained between individual due process rights and the rights of potential victims. The decision where to draw the line is arbitrary, unsupported by empirical research, and perhaps politically expedient. As argued later, these inherent contradictions have resulted in considerable confusion in appellate guidance and policy on protective sentencing.

3   The scope of the provisions

The protective provisions contained in the 1991 Act are dependant on the key concepts of "violent offence", "sexual offence" and "serious harm" all of which are the subject of statutory definition.[18] In *R v Robinson* (1992)[19] the Court of Appeal was called upon to consider the three definitions at length. The first relevant issue was the purely substantive one of whether attempted rape was a "sexual offence" within the meaning of the Act. Lord Taylor C. J. pointed out that the narrow definition in S31 (1) confined "sexual" offences to specific statutory provisions and expressly excluded and omitted some crimes which would normally be regarded as sexual offences. It was argued that since attempted rape was a charge under S1 Criminal Attempts Act 1981 and this statute was omitted from the definition in S31 (1), attempted rape was not included within the definition. The Court of Appeal were forced to approach the issue as a matter of construction and after rejecting two contrary submissions held that since attempted rape was an offence under S37 Sexual Offences Act 1956 for the purpose of specifying the court's statutory powers of sentence it should properly be regarded as an offence "under" the Sexual Offences Act 1956 notwithstanding that the defendant had been indicted under the Criminal Attempts Act 1981.[20] Such convoluted reasoning is now no longer necessary following the replacement of the original definition in S31 (1) of the 1991 Act by Schedule 9, para. 45. Not only does the new section cover the offence of attempted rape it also extends to all conspiracies, attempts and incitements to commit any of the substantive offences now included. The other significant changes are the inclusion of the offence of burglary with intent to rape; S9 Theft Act 1968, thus overruling *R v Josko* (1994), and unlawful sexual intercourse with a mental patient by a person in authority under S128, Mental Health Act 1959. Offences committed within the terms of the Sexual Offences Act 1967 are no longer included.

Robinson additionally held that that a "sexual offence" could also be a "violent offence" within the meaning of S31 (1). The broad definition in S31 (1) focused on the individual facts of each case rather than the specified offences. In contrast with S31 (3), psychological harm was not included within S31 (1) nor was there any requirement that the physical injury should be serious. Since the victim in the case did suffer actual physical injury as a direct result of the offence of attempted rape it was a "violent offence" for the purposes of the 1991 Act. In *Bowler* the Court of Appeal held that when considering whether "serious harm" had occurred within the meaning of S31 (3) a court was entitled to consider the vulnerability of potential future victims to both physical and psychological harm. *Bowler* was confirmed on this point in *R v L*, (1994) another indecent assault case, although the court appears to have been influenced by the fact that (in *L*) there was no apparent danger to children outside the immediate family. The definition of "violent offence" in S31 (1) was also considered in *R v Fowler* (1994), a robbery case. In this case D approached P from behind, demanded her purse, and after grabbing her handbag and carrier bag, ran away. Although P was shaken and shocked she did not suffer any direct violence not any physical injury to the person as required by S31 (1). Hence, it seems that the Court of Appeal were prepared to accept that the offence was one "likely to lead to physical injury" in the circumstances of this particular case although any objective assessment would have regarded such a likelihood as highly conjectural. A similar result was achieved in *R v Cochrane* (1994)[21] where the court took the view that where a robbery victim had been threatened at knife point but not physically injured the circumstances could be treated as a "violent offence" for the purposes of S31 (1) provided it was established that the offence was likely to cause injury if the victim had resisted, or, that the appellant would have lost control and carried out his threat if the victim had resisted, or, by accident.[22] It was accepted as fact that the appellant had not formed any intention to carry out his threat and inflict injury on the victim at the time of the offence. *Cochrane* therefore perpetuates the principle established in *Robinson* that the definition in S31 (1) and its interpretation should depend on the individual facts of each case viz. whether the circumstances of the offence led or were intended or likely to lead to a person's death or physical injury.[23] It is therefore apparent that the scope of the definition of "violent offence" in S31 (1) is not restricted to any particular legal category nor is there mutual exclusivity as regards what constitutes a "violent" and a "sexual" offence for the purposes of the Act.

4   The nature of the test

(i)   Procedural issues

The Act is strangely silent regarding the correct approach to SS1 (2) (b) and 2 (2) (b). The main procedural requirements are that under S1 (4), in any case where a court passes a custodial sentence, it must state in open court that it is of the opinion that either or both S1 (2) (a) and S1 (2) (b) apply and justify its opinion; S1 (4) (a). The court must also explain to the offender in open court and in ordinary language why it is passing a custodial sentence on him; S1 (4) (b).[24] There are further provisions in S2 (3), dealing with the length of custodial sentences, which require the court when fixing a sentence in accordance with S2 (2) (b) to state in open court that it is of the opinion that S2 (2) (b) applies and justify its opinion; S2 (3) (a). The court must also explain to the offender in open court and in ordinary language why the sentence is for such a term; S2 (3) (b). What these provisions do not provide is guidance to sentencers in reaching a decision as to whether a protective sentence is appropriate both in terms of assessing dangerousness and the standard of certainty required. It is important to note that once this crucial decision has been made the provisions of S2 (2) (b) are mandatory; *Bowler*, and the scope to mitigate the sentence under S28 is likely to be significantly reduced where the protective provisions are applied. The only procedural concession to the defence was made in *R v Baverstock* (1993)[25] when Lord Taylor C.J. issued general guidance to the effect that if a longer sentence than was commensurate with the seriousness of the offence were contemplated the proper practice would be for the court to put counsel on notice[26] in fairness to the defendant, thus enabling counsel to deal specifically with the point.

Until recently, there also existed a general requirement under S3 (1) to obtain and consider a pre-sentence report[27] before deciding on a custodial sentence and an additional requirement under S4 (1) to obtain and consider a medical report in the case of a mentally disordered offender which remains. In the case of mentally disordered offenders, the court must also consider the likely effect of a custodial sentence on any mental condition and treatment that may be available; S4 (3) (b). Before the 1991 Act this was not regarded as a relevant consideration and it was assumed that the prison authorities would simply remove mentally disordered offenders to secure hospital accommodation. However, no other procedural criteria exist to aid the sentencer in his approach to the initial question as to the appropriateness of a protective sentence. Given the extremely difficult task of assessing dangerousness it is difficult to see why a psychiatric report should not be a mandatory requirement in all cases of protective sentencing. None was considered necessary in *R v Coull* (1993) even though the appellant had a long history of drug abuse and violence related to alcohol or drug abuse. Similarly, no psychiatric assessment was required in *R v Meikle* (1994)[28] where the medical report was equivocal, concluding that "it was difficult to be sure" that the appellant would not offend again. This in itself raises the issue of the standard of proof in addition to that of certainty in the assessment of dangerousness. Although the logic of the argument should be that the standard burden of proof as to the commission of the substantive offence is applicable to the admissibility of evidence relating to the sentencing decision,[29] it surely cannot be the case that the protective element of the sentence should be subject to a *de facto* reverse burden whereby the defendant is presumed dangerous unless he can, in effect, adduce evidence that he will not offend again. Mandatory psychiatric assessment would eliminate this possibility, particularly if such evidence was subject to positive rather than negative obligations as to predicting future criminal behaviour. This would not, of course, vindicate any particular hypothesis but it would ensure that the sentencer is not forced to decide the issue on the basis of no, or inadequate, information and that the decision itself is, in effect, shared.[30]

The range of information a sentencer may take into account in determining dangerousness was indicated by the decision in *Attorney-General's Reference (No 4 of 1993) (Bingham)* (1993).[31] The Court of Appeal considered that in deciding whether the public needed protection from serious harm from the offender S3 (3) (b) allowed the court to take account of any information about the offender. The sentencer can, therefore, take into account any information in addition to that specifically related to the appellant's previous convictions and responses to previous sentences since the new S29 (1) substituted by S66 Criminal Justice Act 1993 presumably does not apply to sentences passed under S2 (2) (b), in common with its predecessor.[32] Section 3 (3) (a) allows the sentencer to take into account relevant information relating to the offences (and associated offences) including any aggravating or mitigating factors. Wasik and von Hirsch (1990), commenting on the 1990 White Paper, suggested that it was necessary to articulate within the definition of offence seriousness the two concepts of harmfulness and culpability in order to sustain the principle of proportionality which was to form the rationale of the 1991 Act.[33] This would involve detailing those factors which would relate to aggravating or mitigating conduct. No guidance on these issues was provided by the 1991 Act and the Court of Appeal has developed its own interpretation of the relevant factors which constitute offence seriousness (see Wasik, 1993, p.56).

(ii)   Balancing the degree of risk and harm

Although it is clear that the prediction of future harm must be made in relation to offences which fall within the definition of "serious harm" contained in S31 (3) the offences referred to therein must be "sexual" or "violent" offences within the meaning of S31 (1). The nature of the predictive decision therefore requires the sentencer to assess the probability that serious harm (as defined) above a certain level will result. In essence, this necessitates a two-fold process. First, the acceptable level of probability must be decided and, secondly, the level of harm must be fixed. It is tempting to reduce this to a formula, as did Walker (1980 p. 89), in suggesting that *dangerousness = seriousness x probability of harm* but this fails to take into account that it is the level of seriousness and probability which constitutes the essential ingredient.[34] The 1991 Act and its appellate interpretation has merely fixed the nature of the anticipated harm. Recent appellate decisions have indicated serious confusion regarding the critical question of determining appropriate levels of risk, anticipated harm and the inter-relationship of these two variables. *Bowler*[35] established the principle that it was unnecessary to establish the existence of serious harm in the past if there was evidence that the appellant may cause serious harm in the future. The facts of the case also indicated that the threshold of the anticipated danger need not be exceptionally high.[36] *Bowler* was not cited in *R v Creasey* (1994), where, on similar facts, the Court refused to accept that the appellant was likely to cause serious harm which necessitated public protection, whilst in *R v Mansell* (1994) the Court apparently followed *Bowler* in accepting that minor indecent assault could involve serious psychological injury within the meaning of S31 (3). These decisions reveal some divergence in the court's interpretation of the level of anticipated harm necessary.[37] It is clearly undesirable that the development of this concept should have become the subject of judicial definition in the first instance. For example, in *R v Apelt* (1994) a protective sentence was upheld on the basis of numerous indecent assaults, a history of similar offences and a prediction of further similar offences. Notwithstanding the predictive issue, it cannot be morally or legally correct that the level of serious harm which determines the need for public protection in violent and sexual offences is subject to such possible *reductio ad absurdum*. In addition to the difficulty caused in justifying sentence length under S2 (2) (b) decisions such as *Apelt* also illustrate the problem of assessing risk under the protective provisions.

The assessment of risk gives rise to issues that are more readily illustrated with reference to the following model:

Figure 1:

Degree of risk	Degree of harm
1. High risk	serious harm
2. Low risk	serious harm
3. High risk	not serious harm
4. Low risk	not serious harm

Figure 1 illustrates the possible combinations of risk and harm adopting a simple dichotomy between low/high risk and non-serious/serious harm. In legal terms it is only that part of the model which deals with harm which is partially defined by S31 (3) that is relevant. As has been discussed the definition of "serious harm" in S31 (3) does not essentially facilitate the distinction between non-serious and serious harm which is problematic and may produce absurd results. However, the greatest deficiency lies in the complete absence of statutory or judicial guidance on the assessment of risk.

This deficiency manifests itself when an attempt is made to answer the following question; where the risk of legally relevant predictive behaviour in low how serious must the legally relevant harm be? - to put the question another way - must the legally relevant harm be more serious if the risk is low? The issue then becomes one of assessing how much more serious is "more serious" than average and what is meant by "low risk"? One way of attempting to resolve this dilemma would be to accept the definition of legally relevant harm (whilst recognising the limitations in its assessment) and move to a position which gives greatest weight to the seriousness of the harm to the public likely to be caused by the offender rather than the magnitude or seriousness of the risk that the offence will be repeated. Such appears to be the approach adopted by the Court of Appeal in *Creasey*. The appellant had pleaded guilty to three counts of indecent assault on a male and received a sentence of five years' imprisonment. He had a number of previous convictions involving unlawful sexual intercourse with a female under thirteen and indecent assault on a male. The latter counts were very similar to the present offences. The trial judge had the benefit of three relevant reports; a probation report, a probation report from an officer specialising in sexual therapy and a report from a clinical psychologist. The reports indicated that the appellant was of paedophilic orientation and unlikely to respond to any treatment available in the community. The Court of Appeal determined that the first issue concerned whether the initial sentence was justified by the intrinsic nature of the offence. Having concluded that it was not, notwithstanding aggravating factors, the Court proceeded to decide whether the case was within the criteria imposed by S2 (2) (b). The court accepted that, although the reports showed there was a *real* risk of repetition they did not establish that there was likely to be *serious* harm to the public from the offender;

> The nature of the offences actually committed whilst
> unpleasant and distressing, and not to be in any way
> lightly regarded did not, in our judgement, amount to
> such offences as would necessitate protecting the public
> from serious harm.[38]

The inconsistency of the factual decision has been commented upon earlier[39] but of greater significance was the Court's assertion that the trial judge had mistakenly assessed the seriousness of the risk, rather than the seriousness of the harm as demanded by the statute.

It is submitted that legal predictive decisions should not be distorted in favour of assessing seriousness of harm at the expense of assessment of risk. If such a decision were to be made mainly on the basis of what constituted "serious harm" the question inevitably arises as to whether *any* risk of serious harm should be protected against? This demonstrates the necessity of quantifying risk and the need to describe what is or is not an acceptable level of risk in relation to a given category of harm (see outcomes 2 and 3 in Figure 1). The *Creasey* position is essentially that the potential seriousness of the predicted future harm outweighs the need to accurately predict the probability of harm. It is essentially a reductivist position since it accepts that there are certain sorts of harm against which precautions are ultimately justifiable no matter what the rights of the potential offender might be. This is, of course, an extreme view the opposite of which would asset the unjustifiable nature of any punishment for crimes which have not yet been committed (Walker, 1985, Ch. 20). Nevertheless, it has long been recognised (Floud and Young, 1981, Ch. 1) that some assessment of dangerousness is as inescapable as the need for penal sanctions on the basis that public protection demands it. Administrators and penal agents must, therefore, ensure that such assessments are made and administered as justly as possible notwithstanding the obvious shortcomings of predictive methodology.[40] This pragmatic position necessitates a compromise between the two extreme positions outlined above. If the reductivist view were limited to justifying protective sentences only where some defined serious physical or psychological injury were sustained it would represent such a compromise and this is indeed the position adopted by the 1991 Act protective provisions. However, it is still a position which concentrates on the nature of the harm without consideration being given to the moral decision to dispense with individual offender's rights. The compromise position on the question of individual rights is between the view that holds that a low risk of future harm justifies precautions against an offender even though this entails loss of liberty and hardship and that view which holds that only reasonable certainty of future harm really justifies protective sentences. The compromise view can be distilled to produce an argument concerning the acceptable level of probability of future harm which is essentially an argument about acceptable levels of risk. For example, Bottoms and Brownsword[41] argued from a position that regarded protective sentences as a wrongful violation of offender's rights justifiable only where a "vivid danger" presented itself (Bottoms and Brownsword in Henton (ed.), 1983). the concept of "vividness" took account not only of the seriousness of the harm but also the frequency of the expected harm, its perceived immediacy and its perceived certainty in terms of probability.[42]

Actuarial predictive methods give some precision to the assessment of dangerousness in estimating the probability that an individual will cause future harm by assigning the individual to a risk group on the basis of certain measurable factors whilst clinical methodology attempts to achieve a comparable objective[43] by examining all relevant information about the offender as a basis for its predictions. It is significant that Cocozza and Steadman (1976) found that the factor which most influenced psychiatrists in their predictive decisions was the seriousness of the offence for which the offender had been arrested. The fact that psychiatric reports are instrumental in protective sentencing decisions together with the need to concentrate on assessment of seriousness of harm imposed by the 1991 Act sentencing provisions may explain the court's emphasis on the seriousness of the anticipated harm at the expense of risk assessment. As made clear in *Creasey*, it is not the seriousness of the risk but the seriousness of the harm which S31 (3) required to be assessed. The issue is essentially derived from what is the appropriate sentence for the *offence*. It may also be significant that the Court has adopted, by analogy, its own interpretation of the meaning of the words "from serious harm" as they appear in S41 Mental Health Act 1983[44] which deals with the criteria to be used in the making of a Restriction Order. In *R v Birch* (1989), Mustill L.J. held that the sentencer's assessment of the offender's anticipated future behaviour should be concerned not with the seriousness of the risk that the offender will re-offend but rather with the risk that if he does so the public will suffer serious harm. His Lordship stated (p. 213):

> The harm in question need not, in our view, be limited to personal injury. Nor need it relate to the public in general, for it would in our judgement suffice if a category of persons or even a single person, were adjudged to be at risk: although the category of person so protected would no doubt exclude the offender himself.[45] Nevertheless, the potential harm must be serious, and a high possibility of a recurrence of minor offences will no longer be sufficient.

Hence, Mustill L.J. was prepared to recognise the significance of low risk in this context although priority was reserved for the assessment of the harm rather than the risk. As has been argued, assessing potential risk is equally

96

as important as identifying the relevant harm. Risk should not simply be regarded as a *factor* to be taken into account.[46] This approach was evident in *Creasey* which paradoxically demonstrated that it would be facile to suggest that sentencers do not necessarily take the assessment of risk into account. However, Ebsworth J. referred to a "real risk" of repetition and such imprecise phraseology in common with "serious risk" or "not likely" when referring to anticipated future conduct simply serves to illustrate how the balance of judicial interpretation is weighed in favour of the assessment of future harm.

The deficiencies described are compounded by the principle, clearly established by *Bowler*, that it is not necessary to show that the appellant has caused serious harm in the past if there is evidence to indicate that he may do so in the future. The vulnerability of potential victims is an important consideration in assessing serious harm.[47] Clearly, in such cases the potential for serious harm *may* be based on present assessment and need not be supported by evidence relating to past behaviour. This suggests an even weaker basis from which to infer potential future behaviour than actuarial and predictive assessments which do rely on past behaviour and are notoriously unreliable. It is suggested that this constitutes a further erosion of offenders' rights at the expense of those of victims since public protection is achieved on the basis of a lesser standard of probability assessment. The principle in *Bowler* was evident in *L*[48] although the Court distinguished *Bowler* on the basis that there were a number of previous convictions for similar offences in that case, a factor which was absent in *L*. Nevertheless, it is evident that these cases illustrate an uncertainty and ambivalence in the standard of certainty required for the assessment of dangerousness by the Court of Appeal. The policy described appears consistent with that originally elaborated by the Government during the passage of the Criminal Justice Bill 1991 through the House of Commons by the then Home Office Minister, Mr John Patten.[49]

The potential therefore exists for offenders to receive protective sentences where the present offence(s) is not so serious as to justify a custodial sentence, where they do not have previous convictions for offences of a similar nature but yet they are adjudged to be dangerous. It will be recalled that the 1990 White Paper (para. 3.13) referred to the need to target "persistent violent and sexual offenders... who are a *real* risk to public safety." It would appear that persistence is ascribed to the perceived nature of the behaviour viewed collectively rather than individually and the assessment of individual risk may in exceptional cases be subsumed to this wider objective.

A positive solution to redressing the balance in favour of an equal distribution of risk would be to allow slightly longer sentences in cases involving high risk of serious harm than those involving low risk of such harm. The problem with this view is that it depends on the accurate assessment of risk for fairness and is therefore practically unrealistic as well as ethically unsound. This necessitates early and consistent review of such sentences since the need for public protection is not static and cannot be confined to the point of assessment of risk and anticipated future harm, notwithstanding that this process may be seriously flawed in any event.

5   The length of a protective sentence

Once having determined that a protective sentence is appropriate a court is required to decide the length of the sentence according to the provisions of S2 (2) (b) which restricts the available term to the maximum for that offence. The determining factor with regard to the protective element in the sentence is that which "in the opinion of the court is necessary to protect the public from serious harm from the offender." Section 3 (3) (b) allows the court to take account of any information about the offender which is before it when forming its opinion. The statutory approach is therefore to consider the determination of length of the protective sentence as a separate process from the justification for its imposition according to the principles in S1 (2) (b). As has been illustrated S1 (2) (b) essentially determines the legal basis for intervention and provides the justification for the additional protective element in the sentence extending its basis beyond the simple one of just deserts. Yet S2 (2) (b) purports to allow that justification to be effected without considering the same predictive issues in deciding how much longer than a normal or commensurate sentence a protective sentence should be. The important point at issue is that once an offender has been determined dangerous there is little justification in giving that offender a sentence which is only marginally longer than the commensurate sentence since this will not achieve the desired objective of public protection. Although a significantly[50] longer term was achieved in *Bowler* and in *R v Watford* (1994) there have been a number of Court of Appeal decisions in which sentences have been too short to provide any substantial public protection.[51] For example, in *R v Williams* (1993) the appellant, aged 56 with numerous similar previous convictions received a five year protective sentence having admitted indecent assault on a ten year old girl. As is often common in such cases the reports indicated that he was of lower than average intelligence, had distinct paedophilic tendencies and was able to rationalise his behaviour through denial of responsibility. Thomas (1993, p. 980) described the sentences as "falling between two stools" - on the one hand it was too severe to be considered commensurate and, on the other, too short to provide any significant public protection. The correct approach has recently been discussed by Lord Taylor C.J. in *Mansell* (1993)[52] where he suggested that each case had to be decided on its own facts but the sentencer in any particular case had to balance the need for public protection against the requirements of the totality principle[53] which imposed a need to ensure that the overall sentence was not disproportionate to the nature of the offences. Lord Taylor C.J. appeared to suggest that if anticipated future conduct was perceived as very serious an indeterminate sentence may be necessary to achieve public protection and offenders whose offending behaviour was compulsive, untreatable and likely to cause serious harm to the public should be subject to long sentences of preventative detention. Although it is clearly undesirable to approximate a precise test in fixing sentence lengths the imprecision of the Court of Appeal's approach serves to illustrate the false dichotomy created by the justificatory function of S1 (2) (b) and the quantitative function of S2 (2) (b). The logic of this dichotomy may be sustainable in the case of S1 (2) (a) and S2 (2) (a) since just deserts requires a precision in fixing commensurability according to the seriousness of the offence but there is no such logical necessity or practical possibility when fixing a protective sentence, which is outside the rationale of just deserts. It is submitted that S2 (2) (b) merely serves to confuse the determination of the predictive issue implicit in S1 (2) (b) which is in itself unreliable and imprecise. Since the majority of cases do not require particularly long sentences it is submitted that it would be desirable if S2 (2) (a) were applied to them instead.

A further difficulty which concerns the length of protective sentences relates to the fact that an offender who may have ceased to be dangerous or whose dangerous propensity may have diminished.[54] has no right to have his sentence reviewed under the early release provisions contained in Part II of the 1991 Act. The offender must instead wait until he has served half the original term imposed by the Court. By contrast, discretionary life prisoners sentenced for a violent or sexual offence have the benefit of S34 which permits the offender's sentence to be reviewed once he has served the commensurate part of the sentence.[55] The offender may then be released on licence provided the Board is satisfied that it is no longer necessary for the protection of the public that the prisoner should be confined; S34 (4) (b). Whilst this situation persists it would be preferable for sentencers to pass sentences of life imprisonment where appropriate in cases where there is a very high degree of risk to the public of serious harm. The imperfections of the system would however, remain in the case of offenders charged with offences where the maximum sentence is not life imprisonment.

An unresolved issue relating to sentence length concerns the extent to which any discount should be allowed for a guilty plea in a case involving a protective sentence. As pointed out in *Bowler* the mandatory nature of S2 (2) (b) requires the court to give priority to the protection of the public from serious harm at the expense of discretionary mitigating factors such as a guilty plea.[56] Despite concerted criticism of the Royal Commission's proposals to formalise sentence discounts for guilty pleas by allowing earlier pleas to attract higher discounts[57] the Government has now given the proposal statutory approval by the inclusion of such a formalised procedure in S48 Criminal Justice and Public Act Bill 1994.[58] It is not appropriate here to discuss the ethical and due process implications of sentence discounts[59] but it is immediately apparent that the principle itself further undermines the just deserts rationale of custodial sentencing in the 1991 Act. It also creates numerous practical difficulties relating to the timing of any plea and its relevance to the extent of any possible discount.[60] If it were to be accepted that sentence discounts were appropriate in the case of protective sentences, notwithstanding the apparent mandatory nature of the provisions, a difficulty would arise in connection with the second para. of the section which states that the court must state in open court if it has imposed a punishment on the offender which is less severe than it would otherwise have done as a result of accepting the need for a sentence discount. This would require a court to satisfy itself first, as to the nature of the commensurate sentence for the present offence(s) according to the just deserts rationale of the Act. Secondly, to then consider whether a protective sentence is *prima facie* appropriate on the basis of public protection and, thirdly, to impose a less severe sentence in recognition of a sentence discount procedure which arguably, diminishes due process. Notwithstanding the tortuous nature of the reasoning process which would thus be imposed on the court it is by no means clear which element of the sentence i.e. the commensurate or the protective element would suffer reduction or how this would be achieved. It would surely not be morally or politically acceptable to argue, on the one hand, that public protection necessitated a certain length of sentence and, at the same time, reduce that element in the name of bureaucratic expediency. The likely increase in charge bargaining[61] would also distort the basis on which the court could sentence and may result in an increase in "real" offence sentencing together with a corresponding increase in prosecutional discretion. The extent to which these factors would be reflected in sentence discounts is impossible to assess but it may be argued that it would introduce additional issues related to sentencing discretion over which the sentencers themselves would have no control. In the case of protective sentencing it would arguably produce an unacceptable increase in the number of uncontrolled variables in the decision-making process.

6   Conclusion

The analysis of appellate guidance provided gives little indication of the actual use made by the courts of the public protection provision contained in the 1991 Act and it is significant that no material on the subject has been produced by the Home Office research and statistics department.[62] It has been argued that the current provisions were only justifiable in their present form if their use was restricted to cases where there was substantial or overwhelming evidence to suggest that a protective sentence was necessary to protect the public from serious harm. It was further suggested that the interpretation of the provisions had resulted in uncertainty regarding the standard of probability required in the assessment of risk of anticipated future harm and that this has produced a test containing serious ethical and practical flaws. The protective provisions are also logically inconsistent with just desert principles. There is no evidence that the change in judicial approach necessitated by the protective provisions has taken place nor that this is likely to occur in the foreseeable future. In essence, this change requires sentencers to justify commensurability and public protection as different processes in sentence decision-making notwithstanding that a synthesis already existed prior to the 1991 Act in terms of the unified primary decision-making process.[63] There also exists a limitation as far as magistrates' courts are concerned since there will be few cases where public protection could be achieved given the maximum custodial sentences available.[64]

Nevertheless, some system of protective sentencing clearly remains necessary.[65] It is submitted that the way forward in Britain would be either to adopt an alternative system of reviewable sentences or an agreed set of principles for dealing with dangerous offenders which placed them firmly outside the mainstream criminal justice process. In terms of reviewable sentences both the Scottish Council on Crime (1975) and the Butler Committee (1975) proposed a system of indeterminate sentences with mandatory reviews at agreed intervals. At each review the burden of justifying prolonged detention would lie on those who desire the offender to remain in custody. A variant, available in the Netherlands, is for a determinate sentence to be passed in the first instance with any further extension necessitating a court order. The Advisory Council on the Penal system (1978) and the Floud Committee (1981) both favoured semi-determinate sentences without any maximum limit. However, the Advisory Council had suggested eligibility for release after the prisoner had served one-third of the maximum permissible term (under the then system[66]) whereas the Floud Committee had not recommended a minimum. As has been pointed out, these desirable safeguards were not incorporated into the present protective sentencing provisions. The adoption of reviewable sentences would obviate the situation currently existing whereby offenders who have received long protective sentences are unable to obtain any review until they have served half the original prison term notwithstanding that treatment may have reduced their potential dangerousness.

If periodic reviews were required by statute they could be made mandatory on an annual basis, but, it would be important not to interfere with existing administrative arrangements. Such an approach is taken by The Model Sentencing Act in the United States[67] which adopts clear principles in its approach to sentencing dangerous offenders. Under these provisions the court may sentence an offender for a period of up to thirty years imprisonment where either:

1)   The defendant is being sentenced for a felony in which he (a) inflicted or attempted to inflict serious bodily harm, or (b) seriously endangered the life or safety of another and he was previously convicted of one or more felonies not related to the instant crime as a single criminal episode, and (c) the court finds that he is suffering from a severe mental or emotional disorder indicating a propensity toward continuing dangerous criminal activity.

Whenever the court, upon entering the conviction, or receiving the investigation report, has reason to believe the defendant falls within the category of subdivision 1 (a) or 1 (b) it shall refer him to [a diagnostic facility] for study and report as to whether he is suffering from a severe mental or emotional disorder indicating a propensity toward continuing dangerous criminal activity.

The Model Sentencing Act therefore proposes precise definition of dangerous offenders[68] and supplies a procedure for their identification. Both of these elements are conspicuous by their absence from the British provisions. The National Council on Crime and Delinquency also made the equally important point that only a small percentage of offenders actually fulfil the dangerousness criteria. They could, therefore, be accommodated in single maximum security institutions which would concentrate on the provision of rehabilitative provisions appropriate to their needs. The most constructive suggestion from the point of view of the diagnostic difficulties experienced by judicial interpretation of British provision is the establishment of a diagnostic link facility where the offender may be observed and studied in detail by relevant experts to determine whether he is suffering from "a severe mental or emotional disorder indicating a propensity toward continuing dangerous criminal activity." There is a clear parallel here with the making of an interim hospital order in the case of mentally disordered offenders[69] and in such cases a court must be satisfied on the evidence of two medical practitioners that the offender is suffering from mental illness, psychopathic disorder, severe mental impairment or mental impairment. Such an order lasts for a specified period not exceeding twelve days initially, renewable for up to 28 days at a time, up to a maximum of six months. When the period ends the court must either make a hospital order or deal with the offender in some other way.[70] Since the same diagnostic facilities and expertise would be involved the determination of legally recognised mental disorder and the attribution of dangerousness could be achieved within the scope of an interim order along the lines described.[71] The final attribution of any label would remain judicial but the procedure would have the added advantage that the diagnostic process would not be constrained by time limits imposed by the court process or the rules of evidence.

It is almost certainly the case that the present protective provisions militate unfairly against mentally disordered offenders who are more likely to be adjudged dangerous since they are more likely to commit "violent" or "sexual"[72] harm within the meaning of the Act (see Chapter 7). Given the unreliable nature of predictive measures of dangerousness and the extreme vulnerability of mentally disordered offenders in the criminal process it appears necessary that protective provisions should contain adequate safeguards to protect the due process rights of mentally disordered offenders. Relevant safeguards do not appear in the present provisions.[73] For example, as Baker (1993, p. 545) has pointed out, the provisions of S2

(2) (b) relating to the criteria for fixing the length of a protective sentence contain no reference to mental instability.

It is hoped that the scope of the present protective provisions is widened by judicial means should legislative amendment not be forthcoming. However restricted the Court of Appeal may be in its ability to correct the faulty reasoning and mechanistic approach demanded of the sentencer by the present provisions their only salvation may lie in imaginative appellate guidance. For instance, by recognising in *Bowler* that in assessing the possibility of future serious harm a court may have regard to the degree of vulnerability of potential victims the Court has indicated that the definition of serious harm contained in S31 (3) is capable of including such harm as is caused by the supply and sale of dangerous drugs even on a small scale. Such illustrations demonstrate that the Appeal Court has an important policy-making role through its ability to decide how to accommodate a danger in terms of the sorts of harm against which precautions are justifiable. It is submitted that this role is of central importance in the development of sentencing policy for protective sentencing since there is no general agreement as to which harms necessitate public protection. It is also a role through which, in conjunction with the Attorney General's reference procedure, the Court of Appeal could demonstrate that it is sensitive to the needs of public opinion (see Henham, 1994, p. 499).

References

1.   Home Office (1990).
2.   The proposal was later extended to the magistrates' courts.
3.   Section 1 (2) (b) provides that a court shall not pass a custodial sentence on an offender unless it is of the opinion, where the offence is a violent or sexual offence, that only such a sentence would be adequate to protect the public from serious harm from him.
    Section 2 (2) (b) provides that the length of the custodial sentence, where the offence is a violent or sexual offence, shall be for such longer term (not exceeding the permitted maximum) as in the opinion of the court is necessary to protect the public from serious harm from the offender.
4.   See Galligan (1981), p. 304.
5.   Since it is based in retributivism it cannot be equated with a forward-looking general justifying aim such as reductivism through

which individual correctives such as individual deterrence and individual rehabilitation may be justified.

6. See Ashworth, (1989) p. 347; Wasik and von Hirsch (1990) p. 511; *The Times*, 21 and 28 August 1990.

7. i.e. under the principles of the tariff. See Thomas (1979) p. 37.

8. For actuarial prediction see e.g. Wenk, Robinson and Smith (1972), Steadman and Cocozza (1974), Brody and Tarling (1980). For clinical prediction see e.g. Kozol, Boucher and Garofalo (1972), Cocozza and Steadman (1976), Quinsey and Ambtman (1979), Harding and Montadon (1984).

9. See von Hirsch (1986) Ch. 13.

10. A contrary view was expressed by Dworkin (1977) pp. 184-205. Ashworth has argued that Dworkin's view is anti-utilitarian only in the sense that Dworkin recognises that a right can still be infringed if there exists more than a marginal calculation of some benefit. See Ashworth (1979), p. 414.

11. For a summary of the debate see Walker (1985), Ch. 20.

12. In the phrase, "Some offenders will be convicted of less serious offences but the Crown Court will recognise that they are a serious risk to the public", (Home Office (1990), p.14.

13. H. C. Deb, vol. 186, col. 399, 20 February 1991.

14. See Floud and Young (1981). The Floud Committee noted two criticisms in this respect;
"... it derives the risk presented by any particular individual from the fact of his being a member of a statistical class; and this seems intuitively objectionable in the administration of justice. It does not depend to explain his behaviour and leaves out of account much information that may be relevant to the probability of preventative measures being necessary in his case." (p. 26).

15. Again, the Floud Committee was highly critical;
"The case-study method has the virtue that it predicts on the basis of understanding and can take explicitly into account every possible item of relevant information about an individual offender: but it has the defects of its virtue and in practice the assessment is fraught with difficulty. Psychological theory is not as effective as statistical theory in selecting what is relevant and important. Practitioners of the case study method suffer from a surfeit of information of varying quality and relevance which they find very hard to evaluate and bring systematically to bear on the task in hand" (p. 27).

16. This was undoubtedly the conclusion reached by both the Butler Committee (1975) and the Floud Committee (1981).

17. The desirability of basing assessment of future behaviour on past behaviour was accepted in *L* (1994).

18. "Violent offence" and "sexual offence" were defined by S 31 (1) CJA 1991 as follows; "sexual offence" means an offence under the Sexual Offences Act 1956, the Indecency with Children Act 1960, the Sexual Offences Act 1967, Section 54 of the Criminal Law Act 1977 or the Protection of Children Act 1978, other than -

   (a) an offence under section 12 or 13 of the Sexual Offences Act 1956 which would not be an offence but for Section 2 of the Sexual Offences Act 1967.

   (b) an offence under Section 30, 31 or 33 to 36 of the said Act of 1956 and

   (c) an offence under Section 4 or 5 of the said Act of 1967

   "violent offence" means an offence which leads, or is intended or likely to lead, to a person's death or to physical injury to a person and includes an offence which is required to be charged as arson (whether or not it would otherwise fall within this definition).

   For detailed discussion of the scope of these definitions the reader is referred to Wasik (1993), p. 132, Wasik and Taylor (1994), p. 24 or Leng and Manchester (1991) p. 36.

   Schedule 9, para 56 CJPOA 1994 replaced the original definition of "sexual offence" in S31 (1) CJA 1991 as follows:-

   "sexual offence" means any of the following -

   (a) an offence under the Sexual Offences Act 1956, other than an offence under Section 30, 31 or 33 to 36 of that Act

   (b) an offence under Section 128 of the Mental Health Act 1959.

   (c) an offence under the Indecency with Children Act 1960

   (d) an offence under Section 9 of the Theft Act 1968 of burglary with intent to commit rape

   (e) an offence under Section 54 of the Criminal Law Act 1977

   (f) an offence under the Protection of Children Act 1978

   (g) an offence under Section 1 of the Criminal Law Act 1977 of conspiracy to commit any of the offences in para.s (a) to (f) above

   (h) an offence under Section 1 of the Criminal Attempts Act 1981 of attempting to commit any of these offences

(i)   an offence of inciting another to commit any of these offences

For comment see Wasik and Taylor, (1995) p. 24.

The original proposal contained in the Criminal Justice Bill (1990) was wider providing that the court could not pass a custodial sentence unless it was of the opinion "(b) that only such a sentence would be adequate to protect the public from serious harm from him (whether by the commission of violent or sexual offences or otherwise)."

S31 (3) defines "serious harm" as "a reference to protecting members of the public from death or serious personal injury, whether physical or psychological, occasioned by further such offences committed by him."

19.   See also *R v Fleming* (1994) Crim L R 541.

20.   For detailed analysis of this finding see Thomas (1993).

21.   See also *R v Murray* (1994).

22.   It was held in *R v Oudkerk* (1994) that psychological injury not caused by a "violent offence" is outside the scope of the provisions. The narrowness of the definition was confirmed by the Court of Appeal in *R v Palin* (1995) in deciding that robbery committed by a man with an imitation firearm did not amount to a "violent offence" within the meaning of S 31 (1) for S 2 (2) (b) purposes.

23.   This can be seen in *R v Swain* (1994) where a longer than normal sentence imposed on a father for assaulting his daughter aged seven on numerous occasions was held inappropriate since he had not used violence to anyone else and no longer had access to the child.

24.   The scope of these provisions were considered in *R v Baverstock* (1993).

25.   208H-209A.

26.   This answered a criticism made by Thomas (1992) p. 239.

27.   Repealed in the Criminal Justice and Public Order Act 1994, Schedule 9, para. 40.

28.   This trend has been continued in *R v Chapman* (1994), *R v Hashi* (1994) and *R v Fawcett* (1994).

29.   Trial procedure requires the prosecution to serve notice on the defence of any evidential matters it proposes to introduce at sentencing which were not in issue at the trial and that such evidence must be capable of being substantiated under the normal rules of evidence pertaining to trial; *R v Robinson* (1969), *R v Wilkins* (1977). If a sentencer hears evidence following a

conviction to determine a disputed issue of fact he should decide the issue on the same basis that a jury would determine guilt or innocence; *R v Nabil Ahmed* (1984). Where it is anticipated that an issue of fact will be left unresolved on conviction the prosecution cannot include particulars on the indictment even where this might prove relevant to sentencing; *R v Young* (1990).

30.   The benefits of shared decision-making were aptly described by Blumberg (1970)   Ch. 6.

31.   This was the first occasion on which the Court of Appeal had substituted a sentence under S2 (2) (b) for one intended under S2 (2) (a) following a reference by the Attorney General.

32.   There is no indication in the Act or elsewhere.

33.   See also Galligan (1981).

34.   It is, therefore, necessary to be aware of the determinants of the recognised level.

35.   This was the first case in which the Court of Appeal considered a sentence passed by a trial judge under S2 (2) (b).

36.   The appellant had indecently assaulted a little girl by touching her private parts through her knickers. He had previous convictions for similar assaults on women.

37.   The pragmatic approach favoured in *R v Mansell* was adopted in *R v Gardiner and Ely* (1994) where predictions of the nature of future violent offences likely to be committed by the appellant were based on the most serious offences, in terms of damage inflicted or likely to be inflicted, previously committed. However, *R v Samuels* (1995) confirmed the Court of Appeal's decisions in *R v Mumtaz Ali* (1995) and *R v Thomas* (1995) in suggesting that the fact that an offender has committed a serious or violent offence will seldom be sufficient in itself to pass a S2 (2) (b) sentence. It would normally be necessary for any previous convictions to be for similar offences to the current offence although sentences may still be passed on offenders with no previous convictions in appropriate circumstances; *R v Crow and Pennington* (1995).

38.   *Per* Ebsworth J.

39.   See also Thomas (1994), p. 8.

40.   See Floud (1982).

41.   Walker (1985) p. 373 argues that this view is inconsistent as it maintains that once they have completed their punishment offenders should be treated as innocent non-offenders, even if somewhat more likely than another individual to do further harm. At the same time

108

Bottoms and Brownsword argue that those who present a vivid danger are an exception.

42. Walker disagrees that there is necessarily an irreconcilable conflict between the rights of detainees and the public. As Floud indicates, a situation of imminent danger exists where a potential victim may act justifiably in self defence, or authorities act on his behalf to restrain the aggressor. If a vivid danger is interpreted as something less than imminent danger real uncertainty exists as to whether the detainee will cause any harm. Floud does not agree that in such circumstances continued detention of the aggressor is unjustified since the potential victim would only harm the potential aggressor conditionally viz. if attacked. In the case of the potential aggressor the potential aggression is unconditional.

Walker (1985) Ch. 5 p. 19 summarises the four main arguments:-

1. It is justifiable for the court to order precautions against offenders who seem likely to commit harmful offences in the future even when these precautions added to the penalty exceed what the present offence seems to deserve.

   This is the likely view of a reductivist. The problems are:-

   (a) the sort of harm against which precautions are justifiable.

   (b) choosing between custodial and non-custodial expedients (some may have been tried before)

   (c) the probability of harm (difficult to assess)

2. This view regards 1 as too wide and that precautionary sentences are only justified if serious injury to the body or mind is feared.

3. This view regards 1 and 2 as wrong because they accept the widespread assumption that a mere probability of future harm can justify precautions which are bound to inflict inconvenience and hardship. This view maintains that only certainty of future harm would seem to justify long precautionary sentences.

4. This view states that precautionary sentencing is always unjustifiable since it is punishment for a crime which has not yet been committed. Although difficult for a retributivist to justify the main problem here is precautions (e.g. quarantine) are taken in other areas of life.

Wood (1988) recently extended the debate in asserting the following two propositions:-

1.   That civil detention of any person classified as dangerous may under certain conditions be justified irrespective of whether he can also be classified as a dangerous offender. If protection of the public is a reason for incarcerating the dangerous offender, it is equally a reason for the dangerous non-offender.

2.   That subjecting dangerous offenders (and dangerous persons generally) to protective prison sentences is never justified. Since prison or civil detention institutions would serve the end of incapacitation equally well further justification is required to subject individuals to the more stringent measure of prison and none can be provided.

These propositions are defended through examining the contrary views of Walker (1982, 1985) and Floud and Young (1981, 1982).

Wood claims that Walker considers the contrast only with non-intervention i.e. simply releasing an offender once he has served his sentence. Walker does not accept that a retributivist could support civil detention. Since civil detention is not punishment, the objection that the person subjected to it is being punished for what he might do in the future cannot stand in Wood's view. Contrary to Walker's claim, Wood asserts that retributivism can consistently hold that there are non-retributivist grounds for incarceration (e.g. social protection) so long as such incarceration does not constitute punishment. The practice of quarantine does not present particular problems.

Wood also maintains that Walker fails to establish a connection between guilt and dangerousness which justifies prison in the case of the dangerous offender and not in the case of the dangerous non-offender.

Floud and Young's contention that the civil detention of dangerous non-offenders is never justified is also rejected by Wood. He maintains the proposition cannot be defended by appealing to the right to be presumed harmless and the distinction between intentional and unintentional harm. The civil detention of dangerous persons, whether dangerous offenders is not morally on a par with the quarantining of carriers of deadly diseases. Floud and Young's principle of the just distribution of risk is just as

110

applicable in both cases. Floud and Young's idea that dangerous offenders may be subjected to the harsher measure of protective prison sentences cannot be accepted in Wood's view. As both serve the end of incapacitation the damage to individual moral status is not a justification for the added suffering and damage.

43.   For a useful comparison of actuarial and clinical methodology see Walker, (1985), pp. 366-371.

44.   According to S41 (1) a restriction order may be added to a hospital order where "it appears to the court, having regard to the nature of the offence, the antecedents of the offender and the risk of his committing further offences if set at large, that is necessary for the protection of the public from serious harm so to do."

45.   *Quare* when in a case involving drug addiction does victimless crime become crime necessitating public protection?

46.   See *R v L* (1994).

47.   *Quare* whether danger to a single member of the public is enough? see *R v Nicholas* (1993).

48.   See also *R v H* (1994). A tendency to cause harm to a specific individual or group of individuals was held sufficient in *Hash* (1994). However, if the serious harm is likely to be directed at a group (or individual) who can be adequately protected by other means the appropriate sentence will be a commensurate sentence under S2 (2) (a).

49.   See note 13.

50.   Given the minor nature of the offence.

51.   *Attorney General's Reference (No. 4 of 1993) (Bingham)* (1993), *R v Coull* (1993), *R v Apelt* (1994), *R v Lyons* (1994).

52.   Followed in *R v Crow* and *Pennington* (1994).

53.   This is expressly preserved by S28 (2) (b) Criminal Justice Act 1991. The principle (although described as a rule of law by S28 (2) (b)) states that when imposing consecutive terms the sentencer must bear in mind the total effect of the sentence on the offender. The reason for this is that otherwise the aggregate term imposed may be out of proportion to the overall gravity of the offender's conduct e.g. *R v Dillon* (1983).

54.   To the point where he would not have merited a protective sentence in the first instance.

55.   See generally Padfield (1993).

56. These may be of considerable significance in sexual cases, see *R v Fleming* (1994).

57. The proposal was criticised on the basis that it would pressurise defendants to wrongly admit offences, undermine the presumption of innocence and the necessity for the prosecution to prove its case. It was also suggested that it would unnecessarily penalise those who opted for jury trial and could operate to the disadvantage of ethnic minority offenders who tended to plead guilty more often. The Royal Commission recommended that the policy be kept under review to monitor its impact on ethnic minority communities.

58. The section states:

    (1) In determining what sentence to pass on an offender who has pleaded guilty to an offence in proceedings before that or another court a court shall take into account:

        (a) the stage in the proceedings for the offence at which the offender indicated his intention to plead guilty, and

        (b) the circumstances in which this indication was given.

    (2) If, as a result of taking into account any matter referred to in subsection (1) above, the court imposes a punishment on the offender which is less severe than it would otherwise have imposed, it shall state in open court that it has done so.

59. See discussion by Ashworth (1993), pp. 835-839.

60. See Thomas (1994b).

61. See Tonry and Coffee in von Hirsch and Ashworth (eds), (1992).

62. Letter from Home Office dated 4 May 1994. It would be interesting to know what use has been made of the provisions in rape cases.

63. This refers to the making of the primary decision described by Thomas (1979), p. 8.

64. Note however, that S38 (2) (b) Magistrates' Court Act 1980 (as substituted by S25 Criminal Justice Act 1991 and S66 (8) Criminal Justice Act 1993) allows for committal for sentence on summary trial of an offence triable either way where it is a violent or sexual offence committed by a person under 21 years of age where the court is of opinion that a sentence of imprisonment for a term longer than the court has power to impose is necessary to protect the public from serious harm from him.

65. For an argument favouring civil detention instead of protective confinement, see Wood (1988).

Walker (1985) summarised the possible forms of custodial protective sentence as follows:-

1. Life sentences
2. Indeterminate sentences

These give most protection and the releasing authority most control. There is no guarantee of release after a future time but release at some future date can be expected e.g. the English life sentence. A minimum period of detention may be prescribed by the sentencer.

3. Reviewable sentences

Indeterminate sentences with obligatory reviews at intervals; the onus of justification lying on those who want the prisoner to remain in custody.

4. Semi-determinate sentences

Sentences where the maximum period to be served (and sometimes the minimum) is either fixed by statute or stated by the sentencer. They allow the defendant to be paroled before the date on which he must be released.

5. Renewable sentences

Sentences of a fixed length which can be supplemented by an additional period of detention ordered by the court, usually after the offender has served part of the normal sentence.

6. Double-track sentences

Sentences of which the first, determinate, part is punitive or deterrent and the second part, determinate or indeterminate, intended for society's protection.

66. For description and critical analysis of the early release procedures introduced by the Criminal Justice Act 1991 see *Sentencing News* (1992), (4), 11-12.

67. See Council of Judges, National Council on Crime and Delinquency, Model Sentencing Act, 2nd ed. (1972).

68. Note that this pre-supposes that there is no controversy regarding the harms to be covered. For a summary of the arguments see Walker (1985), p. 376.

69. For an analysis of the problems of sentencing mentally abnormal offenders labelled as dangerous, see Baker (1993).

70. Section 38, Mental Health Act, 1983.

71. This would have the additional attraction of minimising costs.

72.   Home Office statistics indicate that offenders subject to restriction orders are much more likely to have committed acts of violence or sexual offences than the normal prison population (Home Office Statistical Bulletin, (1992b) and Home Office Statistical Bulletin (1993d). Since many mentally abnormal dangerous offenders will not be sentenced under the Mental Health Act provisions because of unavailability of suitable places and others will not fall within the legal categories of mental illness established by the Act they are more likely to receive protective sentences. See Ashworth and Gostin (1984), Peay (1989).

73.   The only safeguards are those requirements contained in S4 (1) and S4 (3) (b) discussed earlier which do not provide the necessary protection.

6 Mentally Abnormal Offenders

This chapter seeks to demonstrate how the recent trend towards protectionist sentencing has seriously compromised the due process rights of mentally abnormal offenders. The failure to clarify the rationale for sentencing mentally abnormal offenders has produced anomalous sentencing provisions and it has become acceptable sentencing policy that in certain circumstances a mentally abnormal offender may be given a custodial sentence which exceeds the "normal" sentence for that type of offence.

1   Mental disorder and criminal responsibility

A question on which the law equivocates is whether mentally abnormal offenders should be held legally responsible for their actions or whether their condition is more relevant to sentencing. This question pre-supposes that the criminal law expects all citizens (including those suffering from mental disorder) to conform (for criticism see Morris, 1982). It is axiomatic that the criminal law exists primarily to punish and deter individuals who fail to conform by choosing to commit wrong. Nevertheless, it recognises restrictions on the freedom of individuals to exercise choice (which may include mental disorder).[1] The legal notions of abnormal behaviour which may restrict choice do not correspond with medically recognised conditions (see Ashworth and Gostin, 1984). The criminal law, therefore imposes criminal responsibility if an individual understands (a) the physical nature of his actions and its consequences, and, (b) that it is against the law, irrespective of whether he is medically insane.[2] Hence, the difficulty arises in distinguishing between the responsible and those lacking responsibility since there are degrees of sanity which make the drawing of any legal boundary meaningless, see for example the insanity defence. Further, the insanity defence is linked directly to some prohibited act whereas insanity is not treated as a general condition.

Wooton (1981) took the view that mental abnormality did not in any real sense diminish or eliminate criminal responsibility since it was impossible to comprehend human subjectivity. To classify individuals as mentally disordered or criminally responsible was anomalous and it was impossible to describe when behaviour beyond that which society could comprehend should become attributable to a medical condition. This view was elaborated by Szasz (1960) who postulated that the attribution of mental illness was simply an attempt to provide scientific objectivity to our desire to impose moral values on others. In the present context the most significant implication of Wooton's position was the acceptance of the view adopted by the Butler Committee on Mentally Abnormal Offenders that criminal procedure should aim to be preventative rather than punitive (Wooton, 1981, p. 111). For mentally abnormal offenders this would entail ignoring legal distinctions between normal/abnormal and concentrating instead on their prospects for future treatment. Current sentencing provisions have confused aims for dealing with mentally abnormal offenders and reveal a dangerous trend towards protectionism at the expense of treatment.

2   **The Mental Health Act 1983**

It may be supposed that the Mental Health Act is clear in its approach. However, there has been much argument about the classification of mental disorders contained in the Act which again illustrate the difficulties of reconciling medical and legal concepts of mental disorder (Ashworth and Gostin, 1984).[3]

There is no need to elaborate these arguments suffice it to record the clear emphasis on treatability in the making of Hospital Orders. This is a specific requirement where the person is suffering from a minor disorder such as mental impairment or psychopathic disorder. In the case of an offender suffering from mental illness or severe mental impairment the discharge of a patient is subject to treatment viability. Where the treatability criterion is applied the court must find that it is likely that treatment will effect some change in the offender's mental condition either in the sense that the condition can be cured or remedied, or that it can be prevented from becoming worse. An overriding consideration is that the Hospital Order must be the most suitable method of disposal implying that a

116

non-custodial sentence may be appropriate where there is no significant risk to the public. It should also be noted that it may be appropriate to impose a Hospital Order even though there is no causal link between the offender's mental disorder and the offence in respect of which it is made; *R v McBride* (1972). The proportion of the prison population suffering from mental disorder has continued to increase and it has been suggested that as many as one-third might be classified as mentally disordered (see Gunn, Maden and Swinton, 1991). An important factor contributing to the increase has been failure to meet the Hospital Order treatability criterion which may leave the court with imprisonment as the only realistic alternative. Even in cases fulfilling the treatability criterion lack of suitable accommodation may result in courts resorting to imprisonment (Peay, 1989, and see Ashworth, 1992).

Restriction Orders under S41 are necessarily protectionist since the restriction is added to the S37 Hospital Order not by way of punishment but as a measure for the protection of the public from serious harm. In reaching their decision the court must have regard to the nature of the offence, the antecedents of the offender and the risk of committing further offences if the offender is released. This requires the court to make a predictive decision based on the perceived dangerousness of the offender (see Floud and Young, 1981, Prins, 1990, Baker, 1993). The Court of Appeal gave guidance to sentencers on the criteria for use of the Restriction Order in *R v Birch* (1989) where Mustill L.J. made it clear that a Restriction Order should not be added to mark the gravity of an offence or as a means of punishment. It was also stated that the words "from serious harm" contained in S41 required the court to assess the extent to which the public will suffer serious harm if the offender does re-offend rather than the seriousness of the risk that the offender will re-offend. Seriousness of harm was one factor to be determined particularly in a case where there was a low risk of re-offending but the perceived seriousness of any harm that may be caused is significant.

There may be cases where a life sentence is a realistic alternative to a Restriction Order. In *R v Pither* (1979) the Court of Appeal gave guidance on the choice between a Restriction Order and life imprisonment indicating that in cases where the offender was subject to a degree of instability making it probable that he will commit serious offences if not subject to indefinite detention a life sentence was preferable. However, in choosing between Restriction Orders and custodial sentences in general Mustill L.J. in *R v Birch* suggested two areas of difficulty. The first relates to the situation where the offender is classified as dangerous yet there is no secure hospital accommodation available. Where a determinate prison sentence is imposed it should be proportional to the offence; *R v Hook* (1980) yet there have been cases where the courts have upheld disproportionate terms of custody on the basis that there is no secure hospital place and public protection required it, *R v Scanlon* (1979), *R v Gouws* (1981). More recently, the Court of Appeal have exceptionally preferred a life sentence on the grounds of public protection instead of a Restriction Order where there was secure hospital accommodation available; *R v Fleming* (1992). In cases where the sentencer considers that there is an element of culpability notwithstanding the offender's mental disorder it is permissible to take the view that the offence itself merits punishment and apply the principle of just desert. This may occur where there is no connection between the mental disorder and the offence or where the defendant's responsibility for the offence is diminished. What all these cases indicate is that there are no clear principles to determine in what circumstances a protective determinate or indeterminate sentence is to be preferred to a Restriction Order. It is essentially an issue requiring a predictive assessment of dangerousness based on medical evidence. The only philosophical argument which supports this position is utilitarian which also makes the assumption that mentally disordered offenders are more likely than non-mentally disordered offenders to do harm requiring a protectionist sentencing response. It also assumes that the individual is suffering from a mental condition which is treatable.

Where the mental condition is non-treatable life imprisonment has been imposed in cases where there is no clear medical evidence that the accused was mentally ill at the time of the present offence. If the medical evidence was nevertheless such as to allow the sentencer to conclude that the offender was a danger to the public because of a history of previous similar convictions or a series of similar offences then a life sentence could be justified; *R v Dempster* (1987). In *R v Birch* itself, where the defendant had a substantial history of similar offences the medical evidence seemed to establish that he was not mentally ill but would benefit from treatment. It is apparent therefore that it is those offenders who are on the borderline of legally classifiable mental abnormality who are the most at risk from protective sentencing.[4] The potential abuse has however been substantially increased by recent Government legislation.

3   The Criminal Justice Acts 1991 and 1993

At first glance the Criminal Justice Act 1991 appears to take a constructive approach to the sentencing of mentally abnormal offenders. Section 28 (4)

118

states that nothing in the Act requires a custodial sentence to be passed on an offender and that a mentally disordered offender can be dealt with in the manner which the court thinks most appropriate. New criteria for imposing custody on an offender who is or appears to be mentally disordered were imposed by S4. In addition to requiring a medical report in all cases where an offender is or appears to be mentally disordered unless the court deems it unnecessary, the court must also consider the likely effect of a custodial sentence on any mental condition and treatment that may be available. Before the Act this was not a relevant consideration and it was assumed that the prison authorities would simply remove mentally disordered offenders to secure hospital accommodation. Although S4 may encourage a new approach among sentencers it needs to be accompanied by positive changes in hospital admissions policies and increased health and social security provision since some mentally abnormal offenders are imprisoned for public protection due to the lack of suitable hospital places (Peay, 1989). Failure in this respect may lead to an increase in the previous trend towards deliberate imprisonment of some mentally abnormal offenders (see Woolf, 1991, para. 10.120).

In other respects mentally abnormal offenders are subject to the general sentencing provisions of the Act contained in S1 (2). Therefore, before any mentally abnormal offender may be given a custodial sentence it must be justified according to S1 (2) (a) and its length determined in accordance with S2 (2) (a).[5] However, danger lies in the protectionist provision contained in S1 (2) (b) of the Act. This states that the second criterion for the imposition of a custodial sentence is that the offence is a violent or sexual offence and that only a custodial sentence would be adequate to protect the public from serious harm from the offender. "Violent" and "sexual" offences are defined by S31 (1),[6] and S31 (3) states that any reference to protecting the public from serious harm is to be construed as a reference to protecting members of the public from death or serious personal injury, whether physical or psychological which would be occasioned by future violent or sexual offences committed by the offender. Section 2 (2) (b) states that where the offence is a violent or sexual offence the custodial sentence should be for such longer term (not exceeding the maximum) as is necessary in the opinion of the court to protect the public from serious harm from the offender. Section 2 (3) requires the court to state why it considers a longer sentence is required and explain to the offender in ordinary language why the sentence is for such a term. Ashworth (1992) makes two important points in connection with the protectionist provisions in the Act. First, he suggests that there may be

119

cases which will satisfy the protective provision in S1 (2) (b) but not the seriousness provision in S1 (2) (a). These would be cases involving a relatively non-serious offence on the present occasion with a prediction of serious harm in the future. Secondly, it is clear that the protective element added to the commensurate sentence should be linked to the prediction of serious harm. Although S31 (3) defines "serious harm" for this purpose nothing is said about the required degree of probability. Hence, the crucial question of deciding in what circumstances the protectionist provision may be justified is left to the court. This aspect has been criticised elsewhere by Thomas (1992, p. 239). The difficulty with the provisions lies in the fact that mentally abnormal offenders are more likely to be adjudged dangerous since they are more likely to commit "violent" or "sexual" harm within the meaning of the Act. Although no Home Office statistics have been produced on the use of the protective provisions in the Criminal Justice Act 1991, Home Office Statistics on restricted patients admitted to hospital in 1991 show the largest group had committed acts of violence against the person (45 per cent) and there was a large rise in admissions for sexual offences. Of the 2,143 patients detained in hospital on 31 December 1991 62 per cent had committed acts of violence against the person and 12 per cent sexual offences (Home Office, 1993). Since the borderline between legally classified mental disorder and "normality" is problematic it can be argued that offenders suffering from mental abnormalities, but not sentenced under the Mental Health Act 1983 provisions, would reflect a greater proportion of acts of violence against the person and sexual offences than in the average "normal" prison population.[7] Such offenders would instead be sentenced under the protective provisions of the 1991 Act. It has been further argued that some offenders who should receive a Mental Health Act disposal do not and are instead sent to prison under the protective provisions. Given the unreliability of predictive measures of dangerousness and the extreme vulnerability of mentally abnormal offenders it is essential that the new provisions contain adequate safeguards to protect the due process rights of mentally abnormal offenders. Regrettably, this does not appear to be the case.

There have now been a significant number of cases decided by the Court of Appeal on the interpretation of the protective provisions of the Criminal Justice Act 1991[8] (see further Chapter 5). It is apparent from *R v Bowler* that the need for a protective sentence may be satisfied by a prediction regarding the possibility of serious harm being caused in the future without any regard as to whether there has been a record of serious harm in the past. Further, in assessing the possibility of future serious harm the court may have regard to the degree of vulnerability of potential victims. It has also emerged that the protective efficiency of the sentence depends significantly on the maximum term available for the offence since this provides an upper limit for any protective measure. Thomas (1993) has argued that in many cases the additional period awarded in custody as a result of the special power will be inadequate to protect against offenders who really are a danger to the community. This inadequacy is also compounded by the fact that the potential discount for a guilty plea under S2 (2) (b) may be high. Recent cases have also revealed the anomaly that there is no provision which allows an offender serving a longer than normal sentence under S2 (2) (b) to apply to the Parole Board once having served that part of the sentence which has been passed to reflect the gravity of the offence, in which case his continued detention could only be justified on the basis of a further predictive assessment of dangerousness. This is a provision which is currently available to those serving a discretionary life sentence.

Although the protective provision may be employed without reference to past record there is no doubt that in the majority of cases evidence of dangerousness will be largely based on inferences of future behaviour derived from previous offences. In cases involving a long history of violent crime, (such as *R v Coull*) or sexual abuse of children (as in *R v Williams*) a psychiatric report should be mandatory yet there is no evidence of one having been obtained in the former case. The discretion to dispense with such a report in S4 appears too wide given the obligation to take the likely effect of a custodial sentence into account where a report has been obtained. Given the important implications for treatment of the offender this is an important weakness in the legislation particularly as regards those offenders who may be on the borderline of legally recognised mental disorder.

As indicated, discretionary life sentences are subject to separate provisions under the Act. For example, if a life sentence is imposed on a violent or sexual offender the court must state in open court what proportion of the sentence has been imposed because of the seriousness of the offence under S2 (2) (a). It may be the case that a life sentence is considered appropriate under S2 (1) (a) in any event. What is lacking in the provisions is any explanation of the relationship between discretionary life sentences and protectionist sentences passed under S2 (2) (b) of the Act. The problem derives from the fact that S2 (4) of the Act makes it clear that a custodial sentence for an indefinite period is to be regarded as longer than a protective sentence passed under S2 (2) (b). So when will it be appropriate to impose a normal determinate sentence or life imprisonment for a violent or sexual offence? Baker (1993) suggests that the pre-Act principles laid down in *R v Hodgson* (1968) may become applicable in such cases, in particular the criterion that a life sentence could be justified where it appears from the nature of the offences or from the defendant's history that he is a person of unstable character likely to commit such offences in the future. The extension of the concept of "unstable character" to "mental instability" in later cases suggests that the latter will become an important interpretative tool in deciding when a discretionary life sentence may be appropriate under the protectionist provisions of the Act.[9] However, the problem with the pre-Act principles is that the option of a discretionary life sentence is not appropriate in the vast majority of cases involving a violent or sexual element where the offender is suffering from some mental abnormality. It is also the case that the pre-Act principles treated life imprisonment as an individualised sentence based on the needs of the offender rather than a sentence based on just desert and protectionism as it has become under the Act. This must also be considered a backward step as far as mentally abnormal offenders are concerned.

It is also significant that the Divisional Court has recently held in *R v Secretary of State for the Home Department, ex parte Hickey and Others* (1993) that the parole provisions of the Criminal Justice Act 1991 apply in the case of a life prisoner who subsequently becomes a mental patient whilst under detention (see generally, Padfield 1993). As indicated, under S34 of the Act the continued detention of a life prisoner must be further justified on protective grounds once the penal element of the offender's sentence has been served. It had been argued that while in hospital a life prisoner was not a prisoner serving a life sentence so that if the penal element of his sentence had not expired before he was transferred to hospital he could not take advantage of S 34 and would instead become subject to the release procedures of the Mental Health Review Tribunal. This decision surely strengthens the case for uniformity of review procedures between the Mental Health Act and the Criminal Justice Act 1991.

4   **Conclusion**

It has been argued that there is evidence of an increasingly dangerous trend from treatment to protectionism in the sentencing of mentally abnormal offenders without any corresponding safeguard for the rights of these offenders. This difficulty might be addressed by first re-considering the nature of those rights which should be accorded to mentally abnormal offenders in the sentencing process, see Walker (1985). However, the circumstances in which measures should be taken against those who are judged to be dangerous has resulted in inconclusive debate. The treatability or non-treatability of the offender is subsumed to this wider issue. Further, neither treatability nor culpability have provided an adequate basis on which to determine policy for sentencing mentally abnormal offenders. In the absence of adequate legislative protection the position of mentally abnormal offenders can only be safeguarded by adequate guidance from the Court of Appeal to maintain rationality and proportionality in the use of the various alternative disposals available. If this does not occur soon we can expect to see more mentally abnormal offenders unjustly deprived of their liberty.

References

1. It also assumes that expressions of will can be accurately categorised in legal terms.
2. It is arguable that Peter Sutcliffe would have been classed as medically insane yet he was found to be criminally responsible since he understood what he was doing was killing people and that these acts were against the law. Although he appears to have been suffering diminished responsibility in legal terms the plea was rejected by the jury on the basis of the evidence presented to it (see Prins, 1983).
3. Harding and Koffman (1995) maintain that tracing the relationship between mental disorder and criminality is problematic for two main reasons:-
    1. The basic concepts are open to manipulation and interpretation.
    2. Even if a theoretical framework was agreed on, the character of penal and psychiatric populations does not allow very specific conclusions to be drawn about the role of mental disorder in the emergence of criminal behaviour. Clearly some forms of disorder may manifest themselves in outwardly criminal behaviour. The criminal justice system must identify them and decide on the appropriate moral and practical response. Although there has been much argument about the classification of mental disorders

Harding and Koffman feel it is sufficient to distinguish between psychoses : neuroses : retardation (or impairment or subnormality) and psychopathic (or personality) disorder. Most problems for the criminal justice system are presented by certain types of psychosis and with psychopathy. The terminology employed by the Mental Health Acts is based on broad concepts. In so far as any definition is attempted it is in terms of outward behaviour and anti-social consequences and, in particular relies on the idea of abnormally aggressive and seriously irresponsible conduct. Certain conditions are excluded from the ambit of "mental disorder"; promiscuity, immoral conduct, sexual deviancy and drug or alcohol dependence under S1 (3) Mental Health Act (1983). "Mental illness" is not defined, but may include a range of psychoses and neuroses. Mental impairment and psychopathic disorders are defined according to their result which typifies legal concern for a justification for commital to hospital and other compulsory measures. The mentally retarded person or "mild" psychopath whose behaviour is not crucially aggressive or socially irresponsible is not therefore subject to these procedures and should be dealt with in the community in Harding and Koffman's view. It is clear that specific definition is unwise since opinions change. For example "subnormality" in the Mental Health Act (1959) was replaced with "impairment" but despite wide preference for "personality disorder" the term "psychopathic disorder" has been retained. It is evident that medical and legal concepts are used for different purposes and the translation from one discipline to another is problematic.. For instance, persons suffering from a psychosis, especially schizophreina are usually thought to be "mad" by layman yet many of the well known criminal insanity cases (including M'Naghten) involved personalities diagnosed as psychotic. As far as mental impairment is concerned it is the moderately retarded or impaired person who is likely to be affected by the criminal law. Psychopathic personalities present particular problems. The condition is rarely treatable and their anti-social actions are generally severe. Regrettably, many find their way into the prison system.

4.	The following cases illustrate some of the difficulties faced by sentencers dealing with offenders on the borderline of mental abnormality:-

In *R v Nelson* (1972) the Appellant was convicted of damaging five windows, valued at £10. He had deliberately broken a number of windows at commercial premises a few yards from a police station, intending to be arrested in order to obtain shelter for the night. He had a large number of previous convictions and was described as a socially inadequate alcoholic but his condition did not justify his being admitted to a mental hospital. He received a three year prison sentence with a suspended sentence of three months activated concurrently and a further consecutive term of nine months' imprisonment for an offence for which the Appellant had previously been conditionally discharged. The Court of Appeal varied the sentence to three months with consecutive terms the same. Thomas gives this as an illustration of the principle that a sentence of imprisonment should not be disproportionate to the offence for which it was imposed. Where an offender suffering from some degree of mental disorder cannot be accommodated in a mental hospital it is wrong in principle to impose a disproportionate sentence of imprisonment to ensure the offender is held in safe custody for a long time. In *R v Watson* (1975) the Appellant was sentenced to two years' imprisonment for obtaining a meal valued at fifty pence by criminal deception, having ordered a meal in a cafe without the means to pay. In addition to a record of minor offences and periods in mental hospitals there was a history of "bizarre-behaviour"; throwing things from the balcony of his 10th floor flat, dressing in women's clothes and minor acts of violence. Efforts by social workers and probation officers to assist had failed. The medical evidence was that although the Appellant was probably not suffering from any mental illness, he could not be managed in a non-custodial setting. The Court of Appeal felt that although a social nuisance the two year sentence could not possibly stand and therefore quashed the sentence having heard that "suitable arrangements" could be made. Finally, in *R v Fisher* (1981) the Appellant, who had spent most of the last five years in custody, was convicted of burglary, criminal damage and theft. He had stolen fifty pence from a till in a shop and was discovered to be living in an unoccupied house, the door of which had been damaged by him.

He had stolen some bedding and other items from a cottage in a neighbouring village. The Appellant was described in a number of medical reports as an inadequate psycophathic personality of very low intelligence who was likely to remain unmanageable in the community: he was not eligible for a hospital order and was not susceptible to treatment. It was thought that while at liberty he was likely to commit offences which might be bizarre and sometimes dangerous. He was sentenced to three years' jail. The Court of Appeal felt it impossible not to impose a prison term. The sentences should be commensurate with the offence although they could take into account his past record, his determination to go his own way and the unhappy prognosis for the future. It was necessary to impose a prison term not only to protect the public but to some extent also the offender. Six months for stealing 50pence was excessive and the remaining charges were so much part of the same series of transactions that they should have been made concurrent with one another and merited at most a total sentence of eighteen months prison.

5. S1 (2) (a) (as amended by S66 (1) Criminal Justice Act 1993) provides that the court can look at the offence and all associated offences (or any combination thereof) when considering whether to impose a custodial sentence for the offence on the grounds of its seriousness. S2 (2) (a) (as amended by S66 (2) Criminal Justice Act 1993) makes it clear that the length of the sentence should be commensurate with the seriousness of the offence and any associated offences.

6. *R v Robinson* (1992) decided that attempted rape was a sexual offence for the purposes of S1 (2) (b) and where some physical injury was caused it would be a "violent offence" for the purposes of the Act. The anomaly was partially rectified by Schedule 9, para. 45 CJPOA 1994 which replaced the original definition of "sexual offence" in S31(1) CJA 1991.

7. Home Office statistics for 1991 show 20.6 per cent of the male prison population serving sentences for offences involving violence against the person and 9.2 per cent for sexual offences (Home Office, 1992).

8. The following are recent examples; *R v Bowler* (1993), *R v Coull* (1993), *R v Williams* (1993), *R v Clarke* (1993), *R v Nicholas* (1993), *R v Apelt* (1994), *R v Lyons* (1994), *R v Meikle, R v L* (1994), *R v Fowler* (1994), *R v Creasey* (1994), *R v Cochrane*

(1994), *R v Mansell* (1994), *R v Palin* (1995), *R v Samuels* (1995). For analysis of the Court of Appeal's decisions see Thomas (1994).

9.   *R v Spear* (1994) and *Attorney-General's Reference No. 29 of 1993 (R v Daws)* (1995) establish that a determinate longer than normal sentence of considerable length may be imposed on a violent offender who falls just short of the life imprisonment criteria. The latter may be achieved where the prediction of future violent offences was not sufficient for a life sentence. The distinguishing factor may well be the degree of probability of future offending.

7   Integrating Criminal Justice and Sentencing Policy

1   The policy-making function

There has in the last decade been evidence of a significant change in what has been demanded of the judiciary in terms of practical policy-making. As we have seen, the 1990 White Paper ensured that the judiciary, more specifically the Court of Appeal (Criminal Division), were given a prominent role in facilitating the success of the new Government reforms embodied in the 1991 Criminal Justice Act measures. It became the task of the Court of Appeal to provide the necessary guidance and so "contribute to the development of coherent sentencing practices within the scope of the new sentencing framework" yet, coincidentally, the new policy simultaneously made important inroads into the potential for exercising judicial discretion in pragmatic sentencing decisions. Paradoxically, at the same time that the success of executive policy was being entrusted to the judiciary the latter perceived itself to be significantly undermined by what appeared to be concerted Government attacks on a range of legal institutions. The most significant public disagreements related to the sentencing restrictions in the Criminal Justice Act 1991, proposals from the Royal Commission on Criminal Justice to curb rights to jury trial, proposed abolition of the right to silence first proposed by the Royal Commission and subsequently contained in the Criminal Justice and Public Order Bill 1993, and, perceived increased political interference in the control of police forces contained in the Police and Magistrates' Courts Bill 1993. Lord Woolf's unprecedented attack on the Government's criminal justice policy in October 1993 was symptomatic of judicial disillusionment with the direction of recent policy initiatives. The main thrust of his argument was to oppose the Government's "law and order" initiative delivered by the Home Secretary Michael Howard at the Conservative Party Conference in 1993 by arguing against the establishment of secure training centres for persistent juvenile offenders and the value of sending increasing numbers of individuals to prison, believing that prison should be reserved only for those convicted of the most serious offences.[1] Although it should be remembered that the judiciary's ability to comment publicly on policy related matters was facilitated by the Lord Chancellor's lifting of the restriction on public judicial comment in 1987 and the appointment of several liberal-conservative judges, by the end of 1993 a considerable number of senior judges had expressed serious concern over various aspects of Government penal policy.[2]

The evident lack of credibility in Government criminal justice strategy displayed by leading members of the judiciary not only had the effect of undermining judicial support for executive policy in criminal justice matters it also served to further alienate the two institutions. Judicial alienation was also increased by unprecedented media criticism of judicial sentencing decisions. The criticism was mainly directed at the issues of undue leniency, disparity and inconsistency[3], and, prejudice and errors of judgement.[4] The most recent and concerted media attacks concerned what was believed to be public disenchantment with unduly lenient sentences, such as in *R v Bray* (see Chapter 2). This prompted Lord Taylor C.J.[5] to defend judicial independence and argue for increased judicial discretion to pass appropriate sentences whilst at the same time acknowledging the need to explain fully the reasons for a sentence which "departs substantially from the norm". It has been argued that "the norm", as exemplified in guideline judgements and the test of undue leniency applied in reference cases under S36 Criminal Justice Act 1988, is deficient in assuming that public confidence is assuaged by principles and procedures which purport to represent public perceptions of justice in specific offence categories. Notwithstanding this argument, Lord Taylor C.J. argued that it was desirable that the judiciary should continue to have an input in formulating sentencing policy. However, for the reasons given, any apparent consensus between executive and judicial perceptions of the future direction of sentencing policy evaporated shortly after the coming into force of the 1991 Criminal Justice Act in October 1992. The main practical issues which increased tension between Government and the judiciary and magistrates following the implementation of the 1991 Act concerned S29 (as originally drafted) and the ill-fated unit fines system which itself became the object of concerted media criticism (see Wasik, 1993, p. 383).

The Government initiated *volte face* in sentencing policy accomplished by the Criminal Justice Act 1993 and the Criminal Justice and Public Order Act 1994 confirmed the accusation that sentencing policy formation has become an essentially bureaucratic or managerial expedient where short-term political and fiscal concerns predominate. Lacey's (1994, p. 534) managerialist analysis of the relationship between Government and judiciary in implementing criminal justice policy has thus highlighted the ways in which recent Government law and order initiatives necessitated a managerialist approach to policy-making that facilitated the concealment of its political content and contributed to its instability. The Government and the courts are seen as "managers of criminal justice as a service" in this analysis with the Government essentially "constrained to respond to 'consumer protest' by simply and almost immediately reversing key aspects of its own policies." Whatever the merits of this argument there is no doubt that present reality sees the judiciary as having retained substantial control over key discretionary elements in sentencing practice whilst ostensibly operating in a policy vacuum. Although, as Lacey argues (ibid., pp. 536 - 542), the judiciary may have been hostages to ideological manipulation and expediency in the short-term she fails to make the point that other factors also threatened the credibility and viability of the judiciary. These factors had an immediate bearing on the judiciary's perception of its own policy-making function and its consequent isolation. In general terms this function would be viewed as that of promulgating principles and facilitating procedures which promoted the judicial role to do justice according to due process. Although some commentators, such as Carlen (1976) and McBarnet (1981) have argued that due process if *for* crime control it cannot be assumed that the judicial and executive perceptions of due process or crime control coincide in value or policy terms. It may therefore be argued that judicial discretion can operate independently from political interference with due process rights themselves embodied in law and protected by the courts.

2   Changes in sentencing philosophy

The consequences of changes in sentencing philosophy on the judicial approach to sentence decision-making have been considerable in recent years. Prior to the 1991 Criminal Justice Act it was generally accepted that both the justification for punishment and its effective regulation were a function of retributivism as the dominant sentencing philosophy (see Ashworth, 1992, Ch. 3). The rationale of this doctrine necessitated acceptance of the principle that retributive punishment should be administered in such a way that proportionality should exist as between an offence and the appropriate sentence. This was logically extended to incorporate the view that proportionality should exist between different variants of the same offence type in terms of gravity in addition to proportionality as between different offences (see von Hirsch in von Hirsch and Ashworth (eds), 1992, p. 207). Individualised or rehabilitative approaches were regarded as an exception to the prevailing philosophy. Hence, the wide measure of judicial discretion then available was exercised within a certain philosophical framework where parameters were identifiable, acknowledged and generally accepted. Although there were inevitable cases of what Walker refers to as eclectic sentencing or pragmatism, these were both visible and preventable within the accepted scheme.

Much has been written about the subsequent development of just deserts theory and its adoption as a framework for the approach to custodial sentencing contained in the 1991 Act (see in particular Ashworth, 1992). It is not necessary to repeat these arguments except to record that the "seriousness" criterion enshrined in SS1 (2) (a) and (b) did not represent the overriding constraint on judicial discretion originally anticipated. Indeed, as we have seen, the 1990 White Paper policy directive anticipated that the judiciary (specifically the Court of Appeal) would implement and develop the sentencing jurisprudence necessary to sustain the Act's main philosophical foundations. As Ashworth (1989) pointed out the advantages of just deserts theory were perceived to include the provision of coherence in the sentencing system, public acceptability and comprehensibility, and, consistent and principled sentencing. In relation to the last point, it was felt that the ideal solution would be to structure sentencing discretion according to stated standards thereby ensuring that discretion would be exercised according to legal principle while retaining judicial flexibility. Although the 1991 Act fell short of introducing sentencing standards or guidelines, as desired by some, it provided a just deserts rationale for custodial (and community) sentences which preserved considerable judicial flexibility.

On the issue of judicial discretion two factors have continued since the 1991 Act to effect a revival of the principles of pragmatic or eclectic sentencing. The first point concerns Nagel's assertion that some just deserts theorists do not regard it as a truly retributivist philosophy in the sense that it is not motivated so much by the idea that punishment is needed but rather than by a desire to reduce the prison population (Nagel, 1990, p. 898). Notwithstanding that this was a justification for adopting the just deserts position stated in the White Paper, subsequent political expediency and managerial necessity produced the piecemeal legislative reforms of the 1993 Criminal Justice Act and 1994 Criminal Justice and Public Order Act whose combined effect was to reject emphatically the possibility of a more enlightened approach to custodial sentencing. Since senior judges had expressed some agreement with the reductionist agenda implicit in the 1991 Act proposals[7] the subsequent failure of that agenda removed a substantial element of the philosophical rationale for supporting the legislative reform programme. The second factor referred to concerns what was perceived as the restrictive nature of the framework for custodial sentencing contained in the 1991 Act. The 1990 White Paper (para. 2.9) had made it clear that the main objective(s) for all sentences was denunciation and retribution. Of secondary importance were public protection (presumably excluding protective sentences), reparation and reform of the offender which would depend on the nature of the offence and the offender. It was emphasised that the overriding consideration was that sentencing policies should be based firmly on offence seriousness and just deserts (sic) for the offender. As Thomas (1979) has described, the pre-Act sentencing approach necessitated a choice between tariff and individualised measures. The choice of an individualised measure could be made where there was no "obvious" (viz. to the sentencing judge or magistrate(s)) need for a tariff sentence and where there was some reason to believe that the offender would respond (see Chapter 2). Such sentences were considered particularly appropriate in the case of young offenders, psychiatric cases, intermediate and persistent recidivist offenders. Section 6 (1) of the 1991 Act related the predominant consideration for the choice of any community sentence as depending on the "seriousness" criterion thus forcing the just deserts rationale to be given preference to any rehabilitative considerations. These events were met by a judicial desire to re-assert spheres of judicial discretion which had been perceived as subjugated by the 1991 Act reforms. The re-emergence of the deterrence principle in *Cunningham* (1993) and the relevance of mitigation to the determination of seriousness in *Cox* (1993) are both notable examples of this trend (see Chapter 2).

The gradual dilution of just deserts since the 1991 Act has been accompanied by a corresponding reduction in the ability of existing criminal justice legislation to provide a framework for consistent and principled sentencing. As the justification for enforced consistency has weakened the

132

judiciary have been able to assume greater moral and legal authority to exercise discretion through pragmatic sentencing decisions. The judiciary has, for example, been instrumental in reforming S29 (see Brownlee, 1994, p. 298) and the abolition of unit fines, both of which have increased judicial autonomy. This breakdown in policy direction has resulted in some adverse repercussions as evidenced by the inconsistent and seemingly purely pragmatic approach to suspended sentences and the interpretation of the "exceptional circumstances" criterion.[8]

Particular issues illustrate the extent to which the judiciary (through the Court of Appeal) is able to prioritise sentencing aims and criteria which have direct policy implications. For example, in *R v Ribbans, Duggan and Ridley* (1994), Lord Taylor C.J. made it clear that where there was a racial element in an offence of violence it constituted a gravely aggravating feature and suggested that although there was no specific offence of racial violence there ought perhaps to be one. His Lordship went on to suggest that it was perfectly possible for the court to deal with any violent offence which had a proven racial element in it in such a way that the racial aspect added to the gravity of the offence and was, therefore, an aggravating feature. The decision clearly indicates a constructive use of judicial sentencing discretion to fill a policy vacuum. Similarly, in *R v Aroyuwemi and Others* (1994) the Court of Appeal decided that instead of using the factor of monetary value of Class A drugs in accordance with sentencing guidelines laid down in *R v Aramah* (1982), *R v Martinez* (1984) and *R v Bilinski* (1987) the relative significance of any seizure of Class A drugs would be measured by weight rather than street value. Applying the mischief rule of statutory interpretation Lord Taylor C.J. held that it could not serve Parliament's purpose if the increased drugs imported continued to result in a lowering of the street price and a consequent lowering of sentencing levels. It would also be unfair to take the actual weight of the consignment regardless of its purity. To achieve an accurate and fair standard applicable to all cases the court agreed the need to calculate what weight of the drug at 100 per cent purity was contained in each seizure. The *Bilinski* guidelines were further refined to allow for sentences of 10 years or more where the weight of the drugs at 100 per cent purity was 500 grams or more and 14 years or more where the weight of the drugs at 100 per cent purity was 5 kilograms or more. Finally, denunciation, deterrence and retribution were identifiable aims in the Court of Appeal's response to the increasingly prevalent and recently novel offence of ram-raiding in *R v Rothery and Others* (1994). Lord Taylor C.J. commented that the crime of ram-raiding was in essence a carefully planned composite offence involving theft of other vehicles before the main theft was attempted and there was almost always serious damage to property. It also frequently involved the offence of breach of the peace. As such his Lordship described it as "an affront to civilised society and an outrageous offence, transcending the ordinary type of theft or attempted theft". The five year sentences originally imposed were thus upheld as "richly-deserved". There are numerous such examples where the Court of Appeal has pursued sentencing initiatives to deal with novel or prevalent offences (see Chapter 1). Although concerned to maintain consistency the Court's approach is essentially pragmatic and normally involves balancing a number of competing or complimentary sentencing aims and objectives.

3 The control of sentencing discretion

Recognised mechanisms for controlling and directing the exercise of sentencing discretion now include the use of guideline judgements, the Attorney-General's reference procedure and specific directions in the form of Practice Statements. The use of judicial review in sentencing cases, as Wasik (1984) and Spencer (1991) have described, has not proved a realistic or effective method of control largely because it is not an integrated component of the sentencing structure. As has been noted, each of the remaining components is deficient for a number of technical or administrative reasons. For example, the number of guideline judgements remains small and, in common with the reference procedure, there is a paucity of guidance in less serious cases, particularly those on the critical borderline between custodial and non-custodial sentences. The reference procedure is further restricted in its effectiveness by the narrowness of the test of undue leniency laid down in *Attorney General's Reference (No. 4 of 1989)* (1990). A number of procedural issues (described in Chapter 2) have also reduced its potential for providing effective sentencing guidance and as a corrective for leniency it is difficult to see the rationale for its separation from mainstream sentencing appeal jurisdiction (see Henham, 1994, p. 512). It would be necessary for the judiciary to regard the reference procedure as part of a co-ordinated sentencing strategy before its full potential as sentencing guidance could be fulfilled. Such co-ordination could be achieved through more effective and frequent use of the system of practice directions issued by the Lord Chief Justice. This strategy has previously been advocated by a number of bodies in connection with restrictions in the use of custody for non-violent offenders through sentencing guidelines drawn up by a Sentencing Council.[9] If issued in the form of practice directions such guidelines would detail the ceilings for different offence types, the amount of weight to be attached to such factors as age, previous convictions etc., and emphasise the need to make repeated use of non-custodial sentences for repeated minor offences. Ashworth (ibid., p. 155) has also advocated the desirability of some sort of judicial principle or presumption that pure property offences below a certain value should not result in a custodial sentence. This was suggested as an alternative to the vague "right thinking member of the public" test in *Bradbourn* (1985) since it could more easily be connected to existing and recognised sentencing principles. Either suggestion could ensure the effective deployment of practice directions to implement Court of Appeal policy initiatives, whether or not supporting executive requirements, providing sufficient judicial education and training was made available.

Notwithstanding, the initiatives described provide no indication of the likely impact of practice directions on sentencing practice and, ultimately, on the relative use of penal measures, particularly imprisonment. It is clearly possible to appreciate that direct legislative changes can influence judicial interpretation and discretion and correspondingly inputs into the prison population. This can be seen most convincingly in connection with the provisions in S5 (1) Criminal Justice Act 1991 (amending S22 (2) Powers of Criminal Courts Act 1973) dealing with suspended sentences and, in particular, the way in which the Court of Appeal has restrictively interpreted the "exceptional circumstances" criteria (described earlier). Nevertheless, it is equally valid to argue that exhortations to change judicial practice, such as are contained in the 1992 Practice Direction do not actually change the judicial approach to sentencing decision-making to the extent that relative changes in the use of penal measures may be observed. Arguments concerning the justifications for imprisonment have traditionally been regarded as essentially related to criminal justice policy issues. It is difficult to relate such justifications directly to sentencing policy. Most obviously, as an example, doubts about the reformative potential of custodial institutions raise questions beyond the purview of sentencing policy. Indeed, the Court of Appeal has made it clear on several occasions, as in *R v Hook* (1980), that custodial sentences should not be artificially extended to allow for the sentencer's perceived benefits of treatment in a particular institution. Similarly, doubts about the deterrent effect of custodial institutions or a belief in their deleterious effects are not issues which impinge directly onto sentencing policy although they may well influence individual decisions. It is nevertheless, certain that sentencing policy is substantially affected by politically motivated criminal justice policy initiatives and to this extent it may be argued that the essential pragmatism of sentencing discretion is a reality which should be retained. This analysis tends to support the view that the size and composition of the prison population is more a function of the total input into the court system rather than a result of slight changes or emphasis in sentencing approach.

4   Sources of tension

This section focuses on issues in the sentencing debate which represent obstacles to the integration of criminal justice and sentencing policy.

1.   We have seen that there exists a disjunction between sentencing principles and substantive law in a number of crucial policy areas. For example, offences against the person all ill-defined and do not deal adequately with relative distinctions of blame and harm in respect of different offence types. The broad nature of offence definition has resulted in those issues being dealt with at the sentencing stage which, as Clarkson and Keating (1994, p. 813) have argued, is essentially undesirable since their relative importance and proof are not systematically provided for within sentencing practice. This disjunction is even more acute in the case of the protective sentencing provisions contained in SS1 (2) (b) and 2 (2) (b) of the 1991 Act since the offence definitions which may prove relevant in such cases bear no relationship whatsoever to the predictive decisions regarding probable future harm and risk that the sentencing court has to make and justify. Although accepting the current lack of standardisation in matters of proof at the post-conviction stage, I would suggest that such matters should be addressed rather than the confinement of blame and harm indicators to the substantive stage as Clarkson and Keating have advocated. To do otherwise is to reduce the impact and significance of the two most important factors in sentencing decisions and, hence, the potential for the constructive use of judicial discretion.

2.   There exists a lack of judicial control over major inputs into the sentence decision-making process. The clearest example of this arises in connection with the highly unsatisfactory nature of the predictive decision regarding "dangerousness" required for the purposes of the protective provisions of the 1991 Act. As seen in Chapter 6, this issue is compounded by uncertainty concerning the legal test to be applied in such circumstances and the relative weight to be attached to risk and harm in predictive assessments. We also saw in Chapter 3 how the perceived narrow range of realistic alternatives available to recidivist drug offenders often causes them to conceal the drug-related nature of their criminal activity. This is merely one example of numerous strategic decisions made

by offenders (or on their behalf) which restrict or quality the information flow to sentencers and necessarily impairs the qualify of their decision-making. However, nowhere is the inadequacy of this situation more apparent than in the sentencing of mentally disordered offenders. Much argument in this area has been concerned with inadequate classification of mental disorders under the 1983 Mental Health Act provisions which fail to correspond with clinically recognised disorders (see Ashworth and Gostin, 1984). For example, "mental illness" is not specifically defined and may include a wide range of psychoses and neuroses whereas "mental impairment" and "psychopathic disorders" are defined in terms of their results which, as Harding and Koffman (1988, Ch. 7) have indicated, typifies a legal concern for the justification of a committal to hospital and other compulsory measures. The expression "subnormality" in the 1959 Mental Health Act was replaced by "impairment" and "psychopathic disorder" retained in preference to "personality disorder". It is evident that medical and legal concepts are used to justify different purposes and the inadequacy of the legal classificatory system serves as a framework for sentencing decisions. For instance, a general distinction is made between "mental impairment" and "psychopathic disorders" of the personality on the basis that the latter are generally less treatable and the actions more anti-social yet the causal influence of mental disorder on criminal behaviour in general is not readily understood. It is also apparent that the insanity defence fails adequately to distinguish between the responsible and those lacking responsibility (see Clarkson and Keating, 1994, pp. 373-381). The dilemma for those who sentence most mentally abnormal offenders based on such inadequate information concerns the assumption that sentencing aims are similar for the mentally disordered as for the legally responsible. This view in turn emanates from a position which equates the behaviour of the mentally disordered with the "rational" legally responsible individual when assumptions are made about the likely future behaviour of individuals. For example, an assumption may be made that the fact an individual has already behaved violently means he is more likely to repeat this behaviour if mentally disordered. In this connection it is difficult not to agree with Wootton (1981) that the classification of individuals as either mentally disordered or criminally responsible not only produces anomalies but attempts the impossible   A further illustration is provided by the judgement in *R v Birch* (1989) in which Mustill L.J. purported to lay down guidelines on the choice between a restriction order and a custodial sentence where the offender is dangerous. As part of the relevant guidance sentencers may be required to distinguish between dangerous offenders whose offences display an element of culpability despite their mental disorder and offenders whose responsibility for the offence is diminished although there is no connection between the mental disorder and the offence. The distinction is crucial in that a hospital order with restriction is to be preferred in the latter case; *R v Mbatha* (1985).

3.   It has been argued that a clear distinction needs to be drawn between the control and restriction of judicial discretion. Current sentencing practice has restricted judicial discretion in the sense of requiring that the justifications for custodial and community sentences are those presented by law. We have seen, however, that the only control within that framework is that provided by the Court of Appeal itself in its appellate jurisdiction. This jurisprudence merely provides corrective guidance on matters concerning the correct approach to particular sentencing problems. The issue of the desirable extent of judicial discretion thus remains an unanswered and much debated problem which presents a continuing source of tension between the executive, legislative and judiciary. To the extent that judicial discretion remains intact it enables the judiciary to make moral judgements about the nature of culpability and harm which some commentators feel should be subject to uniformity and precision rather than left to subjective assessment. Alternatively, it can be argued that the subjective decisions involved in sentencing concern matters of specific detail relevant to the present offence and offender which do not impinge on wider ethical questions affecting the moral limits of the criminal law. A secondary issue is that such moral iniquity contributes substantially to sentencing inconsistency and disparity and is consequently undesirable for that reason alone. The moral dilemma produced by such arguments is capable of resolution in philosophical terms by drawing a distinction between retributivism and utilitarianism but, as we shall see in the concluding section, the debate has been largely conducted at the practical policy level.

4.   Both executive and judicial sentencing policy have largely ignored the public perception of criminal justice issues. The potential dangers inherent in continuing to do so have been highlighted in connection with the operation of the undue leniency test under the Attorney-General's reference procedure. The case of so-called drink-drive killers serves to provide an illustration of the nature of the equivocal judicial response to increased public pressure. Guidance was first issued in post-1991 cases by the Court of Appeal in *Attorney General's Reference (No. 24 of 1993) (Wernet)* (1993). Lord Taylor C.J. made it clear that, although in exceptional cases when drivers were just over the limit and there was strong mitigation a non-custodial sentence was possible, "in other cases a prison

sentence is required to punish the driver, to deter others from drinking and driving, and to reflect the abhorrence of deaths being caused by drivers with excess alcohol". He went on to emphasise that in the very worst cases, such as racing along the highway and where the driver denied the offence, guilty motorists should face sentences near the maximum permitted. The gravity with which the Court of Appeal viewed such offences was further reinforced by Lord Taylor C.J. in *Attorney General's Reference (No. 45 of 1994) (Wing)* (1995) where first instance decisions on sentences were described as "wholly inadequate", insufficient regard having been paid to the aggravating factor of high alcohol consumption. Again, Lord Taylor C.J. in *Attorney General's Reference (No. 22 of 1994) (Nevison)* (1995) stated that the public would be outraged at the low sentence passed at first instance in a case where the defendant had caused the deaths of two lorry drivers while more than three times over the legal limit. In quadrupling the sentence from fifteen months to five years' imprisonment the Lord Chief Justice was evidently attempting to convey to the judiciary the necessity for harsher sentences in such cases, although it should be noted that the defendant had previous convictions for drink-driving and was driving at excessive speed. Judicial exhortations to increase sentence levels in the case of other offences are not difficult to find. The offence of rape provides another illustration. It is apparent that recent criminal statistics demonstrate significant increases in reported cases of rape and there is increased public concern in respect of rape and increased numbers of individuals serving custodial sentences for rape.[10] Nevertheless, despite a refinement of the *Billam* (1986) guidelines Robertshaw (1994, p. 343) has revealed substantial inconsistencies in the sentencing of rapists and research by Ranyard, Hebenton and Pease (1994) points to confusion in the approach as to how and when aggravating and mitigating factors specified in *Billam* should affect sentence length in rape cases. It is significant that there is no reliable information available detailing the actual role of previous convictions in sentencing rapists and I would argue that the acute public concern surrounding this offence is an important factor in the justification for cumulative sentencing principles to be applied in rape cases to reflect the proportionate impact of the totality of the offender's relevant previous convictions. Whatever the merits of this argument, there is no doubt that judicial perception of the borderline of public tolerance regarding specific offences remains a constant source of tension in an era when judicial adaptation to cultural and moral change is expected to be reflected in sentencing decisions much more quickly than in bygone eras.

5   Conclusions

The sources of tension in the sentencing system described in the preceding section do not present or suggest solutions that are immediately practical and realistic. The integration of criminal justice and sentencing policy may be more easily accomplished if substantive law and sentencing principles were made to correspond more specifically (see Lacey, Wells and Meure, (1990). However, as Lacey has argued (Lacey in Dennis (ed.) 1987, p. 221), it is also imperative that the existing safeguards and controls aimed at promoting certainty and consistency in substantive principles are also implemented at the post-conviction stage. Ashworth (1983, pp. 91-96) has suggested that the rules of evidence should be extended to the determination of the factual basis for sentence particularly in respect of the criminal burden and standard of proof. If these criticisms and suggestions are accepted they do not address the more intractable issue of deciding on what philosophical basis moral concerns relating to the assessment of culpability, commensurability and harm are to be apportioned between substantive law and sentencing principles. These fundamental decisions as to what should inform policy will ultimately lead to, and be determined by, political and bureaucratic expediency. This inevitably forces us to address the issue of the acceptance of criminal law values as intrinsically rational and uncontroversial. Lacey has described this as the external critique (Lacey in Dennis (ed., 1987, p. 227) and it is exemplified in criticism by Wells[11] and Nelken[12] questioning the fundamental wisdom of accepting the legitimating ideology of the criminal law and viewing it rather as a reflection of conflicting values and competing goals characteristic of the criminal justice system as a whole. Nelken is surely correct in asserting (Nelken in Dennis (ed.), 1987, p. 139) that the crucial point is to recognise and describe the sources from which the criminal law derives its authority and, therefore, correspondingly what legitimates it. McBarnet (1981) thus argues[13] the appeals process not only upholds the legitimacy of the substantive criminal law but the procedures of legality as well. The rhetoric of justice provides considerable flexibility which is important in maintaining the ideology of justice.

Arguments concerning the significance of the legitimating ideology may be theoretically perceptive but they do not go further than to recognise the existence and importance of competing ideological positions and the fact of their manipulation for political purposes in the formulation of criminal justice policy. Political pragmatism therefore dictates the emergence of the prevailing interpretation of the justice concept, as evidenced by the ascent of just deserts theory during the 1970s and 1980s. The same pragmatism will similarly dictate the extent to which judicial control through discretionary processes is retained. As we saw earlier, lack of information control over major inputs into the discretionary process produces substantial anomalies in sentencing decisions. The reduction, restriction or elimination of such discretion is a much debated issue.[14] Nevertheless, the articulation of guideline factors, many derived from sentencing principles (where they exist), already influences the exercise of discretion in the Magistrates' Association Sentencing Guidelines (1993) within the existing framework of criminal justice legislation. Greater appellate control could be achieved in respect of the problem areas identified by a requirement that agreed guideline factors are more clearly specified and explained with a recognition that there should be eventual concordance between guideline substantive and sentencing factors. Although the latter point necessitates a major policy change the former does not. Instead, it requires specific judicial acceptance of a process whereby pre-determined specific factors receive comment and explanation. These factors would be specified in the case of all offence categories and failure to adhere to the mandatory procedure could form the basis of an appeal. An example of the distribution of relevant factors in the case of violent offences is provided in Figure 1.

Figure 1 : Suggested guideline factors

Offence category	Degree of harm	Degree of violence	Mental attitude	Criminal history	Mitigating factors
(Non-legalistic)	Very serious injury	Severe	Planned	Related offences	Provocation
Assault		Serious			
	Serious injury		Deliberate	Mixed	Duress offences
	Moderate harm		Impulsive offences	Unrelated	Mental
		Moderate			
	Minimal injury			No record	
		Minimal			

Note: The assessment of harm as an aspect of crime seriousness is considered by von Hirsch and Jareborg (1991) whose approach is to grade the living standard and impact of the completed harm and then discount the result to take account of threat and risk. Clarkson and Keating, however, proceed on the basis

141

that both blame and harm should receive equal emphasis. The matter is discussed in detail by Ashworth (1991), Ch. 2) and (1992, Chs. 3 and 4). There are issues of enormous complexity involved if it were proposed to construct weighted sentencing guidelines. My suggestion is to ensure articulation and explanation of specific factors not to control judicial discretion. It is to promote consistency of approach. Judges would in effect be provided with guidelines similar to those issued by the Magistrates' Association which would list the factors identified (and to be considered) for each offence in a more detailed form indicating the likely impact of such factors from existing appellate guidance. No "entry point" would be suggested, nor would any specific discount be recommended in respect of a guilty plea, although examples of past practice would be cited. Since it is not legal interpretative skill but subjective discretion which is an issue in most cases the procedure would have the added advantage of reducing delay.

It should be noted that what is advocated amounts to a methodology for a rationalisation and standardisation of sentencing approach and not sentencing guidelines in the sense that relevant factors are weighted. Hence, judicial discretion would be restricted since the consideration of stated factors would be regarded as mandatory. Consistency would be achieved since adherence to procedure and consideration of factors would be entirely visible and correctable where under the present system the esoteric nature of much appellate sentencing guidance and the lack of jurisprudential rigour often makes sentencing an inexact science and certainly not an "art".[15]

Political pragmatism may also ultimately force sentencing policy to be informed by the realisation that the general public no longer perceives state institutions as necessarily protecting the integrity of the person or property. If the moral authority of the state is so weakened it may be appropriate to discuss the wider context in which sentencing policy operates and examine its perceived social welfare concerns (see Hudson (1987), Lacey (1988) and Braithwaite and Pettit, 1990). Such concerns are beyond the scope of a book which examines the scope and operation of sentencing policy in specific offence categories but they are clearly relevant to the debate concerning the future direction of criminal justice policy and social policy as a whole. Within the sentencing policy context the weakening of state moral authority and social cohesion may be translated into a perceived erosion of due process rights. The instrumental role of the judiciary in this process may be both obvious and inevitable yet, as I have argued, asserting judicial independence and discretionary control may be one method whereby citizens can achieve protection from the abuse of state power perhaps through the implementation of a limited Bill of Rights. Such a course of action only becomes necessary if the link between the formation of criminal justice policy and sentencing policy is irrevocably severed and in such circumstances the passage of enabling legislation itself become problematic.

In the meantime, the relationship between criminal justice and sentencing policy must be subject to constant scrutiny and measures taken (by the Court of Appeal) to ensure the integrity, consistency and rapid development of appellate guidance.

References

1. See *The Times* 14 October 1993 for extensive comment on Lord Woolf's speech.

2. In addition to Lord Taylor and Lord Woolf the following are described in *The Times* 14 October 1993 as either more liberal or outspoken than their predecessors; Sir Thomas Bingham, Master of the Rolls, Lord Browne-Wilkinson, Lord Lloyd, Lord Nolan, Lord Justice Butler-Sloss, Mr Justice Brooke, Lord Farquharson.

3. See extensive comment in *The Times*, 27 and 28 June 1994.

4. A summary of some of the best known examples was provided in *The Sunday Times* 13 June 1993.

5. See *The Times* 27 June 1994.

6. For example, Ashworth (1992, pp. 319-326) put forward a detailed case for a Sentencing Council "charged with the task of developing and keeping under review a corpus of coherent sentencing guidance for the Crown Court and magistrates' courts". (p. 320).

7. For example, Lord Woolf in his speech to the New Assembly of Churches, London on 13 October 1994.

8. Section 5 (1) Criminal Justice Act 1991 substituted new subsections for S22 (2) Powers of the Criminal Courts Act 1973 which required the case to be one in which a sentence of imprisonment would have been appropriate even without the power to suspend the sentence; S2 (2) and that the exercise of that power can be justified by the exceptional circumstances of the case; S2 (b). These provisions were more restrictive than their predecessors since the offence had to be judged as "appropriate" in the sense of justifying a custodial sentence under the new Act (i.e. on "seriousness" grounds) on the basis that no circumstances justifying suspicion existed. Earlier cases applying the new provisions, such as *R v Okinikan* (1993), *R v Sanderson* (1993), *R v Lowery* (1993) appeared to narrow the range of circumstances which might be considered "exceptional". This trend was continued in *R v Ullah Khan* (1993) leading Thomas to conclude in his commentary on *R v Bradley* (1994) that the criteria had become meaningless and should

9.   be removed. Thomas suggested that the confusion was leading to immediate prison sentences being passed where previously suspended sentences would have been regarded as appropriate.

9.   The call for a co-ordinated strategy was recently repeated by Ashworth (1994).

10.   For example, Home Office (1994) statistics indicate that recorded rape cases rose 12 per cent in 1993 to 4,631 compared to 1300 in 1983 and 4,142 in 1992.

11.   Wells (1986) criticises the Code Report as it does not help in considering what sort of functions we expect the criminal law to perform. It should address those issues because codification is not the same thing as consolidation. Wells asserts that a restatement, rationalisation or systemisation in itself involves a political choice. The Code's choice is to rely on existing fundamental principles. But the Code does not measure its proposals against any explicitly stated principles as we are all assumed to understand and accept them. A value consensus in society is assumed. The report fails to acknowledge that acceptance of the *status quo* is a political choice. Acceptance of the principle that the law affords more protection to property than it does to the person is too simplistic. A connection between the mental element (a subjectivist view in offences against the person and an objectivist view in offences against property) and protection prevails. This ignores other criminal justice processes which affect the guilt issue e.g. plea bargaining, previous convictions. Wells claims that the model accepts a proposition that property does not represent power and that we possess a legal order which provides justice and equality to all. This is not so as privilege and wealth are maintained through the criminal law. Wells provides two examples:

     1.   prosecution policies are class biased e.g. the police usually prosecute, the Factory Inspectorate generally caution.

     2.   crimes of corporations have been marginalised by setting up special regulatory schemes and enforcement agencies. The Code segregates those offences which are important to all e.g. road traffic and those only relevant to a specialised clientele. Many technical regulations relating to road traffic are omitted. Wells maintains those might be very important causal factors in huge numbers of deaths annually from road accidents as compared with unlawful homicide. The case for excluding some categories of offence is not made out. Wells describes how the use of strict

liability in both road traffic and corporate regulation has facilitated the argument they are not real crimes and separated them from the bulk of offences. The Code's persistence with an individualistic model of offenders has also ensured that the harms which corporations and businesses cause are defined differently. The social construction of violence does not allow for the concept of corporate violence. Violence is constructed as an interpersonal act of aggression and committed by individuals not corporations. The Code takes the view that codification will lead to more consistency and certainty in the law. Wells disagrees, maintaining that interpretation is contingent displaying too much faith in judges. This makes interpretation culture specific. The Code will not necessarily make law more accessible and comprehensible. Lawyer's skills of statutory construction will still be required and sheer bulk militates against this. The Code will not make progress towards making offences correspond with the public's perception of them, e.g. rape.

12. Nelken (1987) is concerned to show that the distinctiveness of legal discourse is related to the contexualising disciplines used in crucial justice scholarship. Much of what is significant about criminal law discourse is lost when it is viewed by criminal justice scholars as an instrument of social control.

There are many legal situations where alternative disciplines may be admitted to offer an expert diagnosis but this is not permitted to displace the legal definition of the situation. Contexualising approaches are important in showing how "facts" about crime and criminality are constructed and reconstructed in the criminal process so as to make them fit doctrinal categories and processing requirements. The criminal law and contexualising disciplines derive their authority from different sources. The certainty, uniformity and consistency of law represent faults in other disciplines. Criminal law derives its legitimacy from commonsense conceptions and judgements which are criticised by contexualising disciplines whose purpose if often to undermine them.

13. McBarnet (1981) describes the significance of the switch of emphasis from interactionist research to seeing "the law as a central focus of research". She suggests three main reasons:-

    1.   The need for information.

2.   the potential influence of the law on its enforcers. She examines the role of formal law in the process of conviction i.e. how it is used openly because of its legitimacy.

3.   Interactionists accounts focused more on what law enforcers *do* rather than with what they should do. This is more to do with the politics of criminal justice.

McBarnet suggests that most studies have a vague notion of the law as a vague standard from which law enforcers are assumed to deviate. Assumptions are made that the law incorporates rights for the accused and the problem is seen simply as one which asks how the police and courts subvert, negate or abuse them. The law itself is not scrutinised. McBarnet asserts that theoretical approaches should examine why the law allows people to be processed as they are by agents of the Criminal Justice system and not simply study the actuality of it. McBarnet sees it as crucial to consider the ideology of the state since the criminal justice process is the most explicit coercive apparatus of the state whereby citizens' liberty is directly interfered with under the known laws by means of due process. McBarnet concludes that Packer's dichotomy between crime control and due process is false. She feels that criminal procedure provides a licence for police to deviate and that due process is for crime control. She sees judges on appeal faced with a guilty defendant trying to argue his way out of his just deserts through legal technicalities. On appeal they must not just uphold substantive criminal laws but the procedures of legality as well. She maintains that the rhetoric of justice in the form of general abstract rules is incompatible with the notion of case law viz. distinguishing, exceptions and interpretation. The flexibility available plays an important role in maintaining the ideology of justice. She refers to the doctrine of precedent which may describe where the ideology of the rule of law is grounded and maintained but tells us little about judicial techniques used to avoid it. Judges can at the same time both uphold the rhetoric but simultaneously deny its applicability in the instant case.

14.   See, for example, Pease and Wasik (eds) 1987, Munro and Wasik (eds) 1992.

15.   A contrary view was expressed by Lord Lane C.J. in *Attorney-General's Reference (No. 4 of 1989)* (1990) p. 46B.

Bibliography

Advisory Council on the Penal System (1978), *Sentences of Imprisonment: a review of maximum penalties*, HMSO, London.

Ashworth A.J. (1979), "Concepts of Criminal Justice", *Criminal Law Review*, p. 412.

Ashworth A.J. (1983), *Sentencing and Penal Policy*, 1st edition, Weidenfeld and Nicolson, London, and (1995), 2nd edition, Butterworths, London.

Ashworth A.J. (1989), "Criminal Justice and Deserved Sentences" *Criminal Law Review*, p. 340.

Ashworth A.J. (1991), Editorial Note, *Criminal Law Review*, p. 1.

Ashworth A.J. (1992a), Editorial Note, *Criminal Law Review*, p. 229.

Ashworth A.J. (1992b), *Sentencing and Criminal Justice*, Weidenfeld and Nicolson, London.

Ashworth A.J. (1993), "The Royal Commission on Criminal Justice (3), Plea, Venue and Discontinuance", *Criminal Law Review*, p. 835.

Ashworth A.J. (1994), Editorial Note, *Criminal Law Review*, p. 153.

Ashworth A. and Gibson B. (1994) "The Criminal Justice Act 1993: (2) Altering the sentencing framework", *Criminal Law Review*, p. 101.

Ashworth A.J. and Gostin L. (1984), "Mentally Disordered Offenders and the Sentencing Process", *Criminal Law Review*, p. 195.

Baker E. (1993), "Dangerousness, Rights and Criminal Justice", *Modern Law Review*, Vol. 56, p. 528.

Bishop N. (ed.) (1988), *Non-Custodial Alternatives in Europe*, Heuni, Helsinki.

Blumberg A.S. (1970), *Criminal Justice*, Quadrangle Books, Chicago.

Bottomley A.K. (1987), "Sentencing reform and the structuring of pre-trial discretion", in Pease K. and Wasik M. (eds), *Sentencing Reform*, Manchester University Press, Manchester.

Bottoms A.E. and Brownsword R. (1983) "Dangerousnes and Rights" in Hinton J. (ed.) *Dangerousness: Problems of Assessment and Prediction*, Allen and Unwin, London.

Braithwaite J. (1982), "Challenging just desserts: punishing white collar criminals", *Journal of Criminal Law and Criminology*, Vol. 73, No. 2, p. 723.

Braithwaite J. (1984), *Corporate Crime in the Pharmaceutical Industry*, Routledge and Kegan Paul, London.

Braithwaite J. (1989), *Crime, Shame and Re-Integration*, Cambridge University Press, Cambridge.

Braithwaite J. and Geis G. (1982), "On theory and action for corporate crime control", *Crime and Delinquency*, Vol. 27, p. 292.

Braithwaite J. and Pettit P. (1990), *Not Just Desserts: A Republican Theory of Justice*, Oxford, Clarendon Press.

Brody S. and Tarling R. (1980), *Taking Offenders Out of Circulation*, Home Office Research Study No. 64, HMSO, London

Brownlee, I.D. (1994), "Taking the strait-jacket off: persistence and the distribution of punishment in England and Wales", *Legal Studies*, Vol. 14, No. 3, p. 295.

Carlen P. (1976), *Magistrates' Justice*, Martin Robertson, London.

Certoma G.L. (1985), *The Italian Legal System*, Butterworths, London.

Clarkson C.M.V. (1994), "Law Commission Report on Offences against the Person and General Principles: (1) Violence and the Law Commission", *Criminal Law Review*, p. 324.

Clarkson C.M.V. and Keating H.M. (1994), *Criminal Law: Text and Materials*, Sweet and Maxwell, London.

Cocozza J. and Steadman H, (1976), "The failure of psychiatric predictions of dangerousness: clear and convincing evidence", *Rutgers Law Review*, Vol. 29, p. 1084.

Collison M. (1993), "Punishing Drugs: Criminal Justice and Drug Use", *British Journal of Criminology*, Vol. 33, p. 382.

Collison M. (1994), "Drug Crime, Drug Problems and Criminal Justice: Sentencing Trends and Enforcement Targets", *Howard Journal of Criminal Justice*, Vol. 33, p. 25.

Collucia A. and Marzi A. (1991), *Criminal Policy in Italy against Drug Abuse and Drug Trafficking*. Unpublished paper presented at the British Criminology Conference, University of York, July 1991.

Council of Europe (1991), *Study and Synopsis of Basic Criminal Law Concepts of Pompidou Group Member Countries on the Prevention of Drug Trafficking and Abuse*, Council of Europe, Strasbourg.

Council of Europe (1992), Prison Information Bulletin, Number 16, Council of Europe, Strasbourg.

Council of Judges, National Council on Crime and Delinquency, (1972), Model Sentencing Act, 2nd edition, *Crime and Delinquency*, Vol. 18, p. 335.

Croall H. (1992), *White Collar Crime*, Open University Press, Buckingham.

Criminal Law Revision Committee (1980), Fourteenth Report, *Offences against the Person*, Cmnd. 7844, HMSO, London.

Criminal Law Review (April 1992 issue).

Dennis I. (1995), "The Criminal Justice and Public Order Act 1994: The Evidence Provisions", *Criminal Law Review*, p. 4.

Dorn N. and South N. (1990), "Drug markets and law enforcement", *British Journal of Criminology*, Vol. 30, p. 171.

Dorn N. and Murji K. (1992), "Low level drug enforcement", *International Journal of the Sociology of Law*, Vol. 20, p. 159.

Dworkin R. (1977), *Taking Rights Seriously*, Duckworth, London.

Emmins C.J. and Scanlan G. (1988), *Blackstone's Guide to the Criminal Justice Act 1988*, Blackstone, London.

Floud J. and Young W. (1981), *Dangerousness and Criminal Justice*, Heinemann, London.

Floud J. (1982), 'Dangerousness and Criminal Justice', *British Journal of Criminology*, Vol. 22, p. 210.

Fitzgerald M. and Sim J. (1979), *British Prisons*, Basil Blackwell, Oxford.

Fortson R. (1992), *The Law on the Misuse of Drugs and Drug Trafficking Offences*, Sweet and Maxwell, London.

Galligan D.J. (1981), "Guidelines and Just Desserts: A Critique of Recent Trends in Sentencing Reform", *Criminal Law Review*, p. 297.

Gaudet F.J. et al (1993), "Individual Differences in the Sentencing Tendencies of Judges", *Journal of Criminal Law, Criminology and Police Science*, Vol. 23, p. 811.

Glynn J. (1993), "The Royal Commission on Criminal Justice (4) Disclosure", *Criminal Law Review*, p. 81.

Graham J. (1990), "Decaceration in the Federal Republic of Germany: How Practitioners are Succeeding where Policymakers Have Failed", *British Journal of Criminology*, Vol. 30, No. 2, p. 150.

Green E. (1961), *Judicial Attitudes in Sentencing*, Macmillan, London.

Gunn J., Maden A. and Swinton M. (1991), *How Many Prisoners should be in Hospital*, Home Office Research Bulletin, p. 5.

Harding C. and Koffman L. (1988) (1995), *Sentencing and the Penal System: Text and Materials*, 1st and 2nd editions, Sweet and Maxwell, London.

Harding T. and Montandon C. (1984), "The Rehability of Dangerousness Assessments", *British Journal of Psychiatry*, Vol. 144, p. 149.

Heinz W. (1989), "The Problems of Imprisonment including strategies that might be employed to minimize the use of custody, in Hood R. (ed.) *Crime and Criminal Policy in Europe*, Centre for Criminological Research, Oxford.

Henham R.J. (1986), "The Influence of Sentencing Principles on Magistrates' Sentencing Practices", *Howard Journal of Criminal Justice*, Vol. 25, No. 3, p. 190.

Henham R.J. (1990), *Sentencing Principles and Magistrates' Sentencing Behaviour*, Avebury, Aldershot.

Henham R.J. (1992), "Evaluating the United States Federal Sentencing Guidelines", *Anglo-American Law Review*, Vol. 21, p. 399.

Henham R.J. (1994), "Attorney-General's References and Sentencing Policy", *Criminal Law Review*, p. 499.

Hogarth J. (1971), *Sentencing as a Human Process*, University of Toronto Press, Toronto.

Home Office (1975) *The Report of the Committee for Mentally Abnormal Offenders*, (The Butler Committee), Cmnd. 6244, HMSO, London.

Home Office (1979), *Committee of Inquiry into UK Prison Services* (The May Inquiry), Cmnd. 7673, HMSO, London.

Home Office (1990), *Crime, Justice and Protecting the Public*, Cmn. 965, HMSO, London.

Home Office (1992a), *Statistics of Drug Seizures and Offenders Dealt With, United Kingdom, 1991*, HMSO, London.

Home Office, Statistical Bulletin (1992b), *The Prison Population in 1991*, Government Statistical Service, London.

Home Office (1993a), *Monitoring the Criminal Justice Act 1991: Data from a Special Collection Exercise*, Statistical Bulletin 25/93, Home Office, London.

Home Office (1993b), *Projections of Long Term Trends in the Prison Population to 2001*, Statistical Bulletin 6/93, Home Office, London.

Home Office (1993c), *Self-Reported Drug Misuse in England and Wales: Main Findings from the 1992 British Crime Survey*, Home Office Research and Statistics Department Research Findings No. 7, Home

Office, London.

Home Office Statistical Bulletin (1993d), *Statistics of Mentally Disordered Offenders England and Wales 1991*, Government Statistical Service, London.

Home Office (1994), *Notifiable Offences England and Wales 1993*, Statistical Bulletin 6/94, Home Office, London.

Hood R.G. (1962), *Sentencing in Magistrates' Courts - A Study in Variations of Policy*, Stevens, London.

Hood R.G. (1972), *Sentencing the Motoring Offender*, Heinemann, London.

Hood R.G. (1992), *Race and Sentencing*, Oxford University Press, Oxford.

Huber B. (1982), "Structure and Changes in Sentencing in West Germany" in Thomas D.A. (ed.), *The Future of Sentencing*, Occasional Paper No. 8, Institute of Criminology, Cambridge.

Hudson B. (1987), *Justice through Punishment: A Critique of the Justice Model of Corrections*, Macmillan, London.

Justice (1991), *Drugs and the Law*, Justice, London.

Keating H. (1987), "Fatal and Non-Fatal Offences Against the Person under the Draft Criminal Code", in Dennis I.H. (ed.), *Criminal Law and Justice*, Sweet and Maxwell, London.

Kerameus K.D. and Kozyris P.J. (eds) (1987), *Introduction to Greek Law*, Kluwer, Deventer.

Kozol H., Boucher R. and Garofalo R. (1972), "The diagnosis and treatment of dangerousness", *Crime and Delinquency*, Vol. 18, p. 371.

Lappi-Seppala T. (1990), "Sentencing Theory in Practice: Implementing the Notion of Normal Punishments in Finland", in Bishop N. (ed.), *Scandinavian Criminal Policy and Criminology 1985-90*, Scandinavian Research Council for Criminology, Stockholm.

Lacey N. (1987) "Discretion and Due Process at the Post-Conviction Stage", in Dennis I.H. (ed.), *Criminal Law and Justice*, Sweet and Maxwell, London.

Lacey N. (1988), *State Punishment*, Routledge, London.

Lacey N. (1994), "Government as Manager, Citizen as Consumer: The Case of the Criminal Justice Act 1991", *Modern Law Review*, Vol. 57, p. 534.

Lacey N., Wells C. and Meure D. (1990), *Restructuring Criminal Law*, Weidenfeld and Nicolson, London.

Law Commission No. 143 (1985), *Codification of the Criminal Law: A Report to the Law Commission*, HMSO, London.

Law Commission No. 177 (1989), *Draft Criminal Code Bill*, HMSO, London.

Law Commission Consultation Paper No. 122 (1992), *Legislating the Criminal Code: Offences against the Person and Criminal Principles*, HMSO, London.

Law Commission No. 218 (1993), *Draft Criminal Law Bill Legislating the Criminal Code: Offences Against the Person and General Principles*, HMSO, London.

Law Society (1993), *The Cost of Default: A Report*, Law Society, London.

Lee M. (1993), "The unspoken sentence? Treatment conditions for drug using offenders under the 1991 Criminal Justice Act", *Criminal Justice Matters*, No. 12, p. 15.

Leitner A., Shapland J., and Wiles P. (1993), *Drug Usage and Drugs Prevention: The Views and Habits of the General Public*, HMSO, London.

Leng R. and Manchester C. (1991), *A Guide to the Criminal Justice Act 1991*, Fourmat Publishing, London.

Levi M. (1984), "Fraud Trials in Perspective", *Criminal Law Review*, p. 384.

Levi M. (1986), "Fraud in the Courts", *British Journal of Criminology*, Vol. 26, No. 4, p. 394.

Levi M. (1987), *Regulating Fraud: White Collar Crime and the Criminal Process*, Tavistock, London.

Levi M. (1989), "Suite Justice: Sentencing for Fraud", *Criminal Law Review*, p. 420.

Levi M. (1991), "Sentencing White Collar Crime in the Dark?: Reflections on the Guinness Four", *Howard Journal of Criminal Justice*, Vol. 30, p.4.

Levi M. (1993), *The Investigation, Prosecution and Trial of Serious Fraud*, Royal Commission on Criminal Justice Research Study No. 14, HMSO, London.

Lundquist A. (1990), "Some Recent Developments in Swedish Criminal Policy", in Bishop N. (ed.) *Scandinavian Criminal Policy and Criminology1985-90*, Scandinavian Research Council for Criminology, Stockholm.

Maden A., et al (1991), Drug Dependence in Prisoners, *British Medical Journal*, p. 880.

Magistrates' Association (1992), *Sentencing Guidelines*, Magistrates' Association, London.

Magistrates' Association (1993), *Sentencing Guidelines*, Magistrates' Association, London.

Mannheim H., Spencer J.C., and Lynch G., (1957), "Magisterial Policy in the London Juvenile Courts", *British Journal of Delinquency*, Vol. 7, pp. 13, 119.

Matza D. (1964), *Delinquency and Drift*, John Wiley, New York.

McBarnet D. (1981), *Conviction: Law, The State and the Construction of Justice*, Macmillan, London.

McClintock F.H. and Wilkstrom P.H. (1990), "Violent Crime in Scotland: Rate, Structure and Trends", *British Journal of Criminology*, Vol. 30, No. 2, p. 207.

McConville M. and Baldwin J. (1981), *Courts, Prosecution and Conviction*, Clarendon Press, Oxford.

Moxon D. (1988), *Sentencing Practice in the Crown Court*, Home Office Research Unit Study No. 103, HMSO, London.

Morris N. (1982), *Madness and the Criminal Law*, University of Chicago, Chicago.

Munro C. (1992), "Judicial Independence and Judicial Function", in Munro C. and Wasik M. (eds), *Sentencing, Judicial Discretion and Training*, Sweet and Maxwell, London.

Murji K. (1993), "Drug Enforcement Strategies", *Howard Journal of Criminal Justice*, Vol. 32, p. 215.

Murphy P. (1995), *Murphy on Evidence*, 5th edition, Blackstone Press, London.

Nagel I.H. (1990), "Structuring Sentencing Discretion: The New Federal Sentencing Guidelines", *Journal of Criminal Law and Criminology*, Vol. 80, p. 883.

Nagel S. (1962), "Judicial Backgrounds and Criminal Cases", *Journal of Criminal Law, Criminology and Police Science*, Vol. 53, p. 335.

Nelken D. (1987), "Criminal Law and Criminal Justice: Some Notes on their Irrelation", in Dennis I.H. (ed.), *Criminal Law and Justice*, Sweet and Maxwell, London.

Padfield N. (1993), "Parole and the Life Sentence Prisoner", *Howard Journal of Criminal Justice*, Vol. 32, No. 2, p. 87.

Parker H. (1993), "The New Drug Users: An Unsuitable Case for Treatment", *Criminal Justice Matters*, No. 12, p. 3.

Pease K. and Wasik M. (eds), (1987), *Sentencing Reform Guidance or Guidelines?* Manchester University Press, Manchester.

Peay J. (1989), *Tribunals on Trial*, Oxford University Press, Oxford.

Phippen P. (1993), "Silent Right", *Law Society's Gazette* 90/35, 29 September, p. 17.

Prins H. (1983), "Diminished Responsibility and the Sutcliffe Case: Legal, Psychiatric and Social Aspects (A Layman's View)", *Medicine, Science and the Law*, Vol. 23, No. 1, p. 17.

Prins H. (1990), "Dangerousness: A Review", in Bluegrass R. and Bowden R. (eds), *Principles and Practice of Forensic Psychiatry*, Churchill Livingstone, London.

Quincey V. and Ambtman R. (1979), "Variables Affecting Psychiatrists" and Teachers' Assessments of Mentally Ill Offenders' *Journal of Consultancy and Clinical Psychology*, Vol. 2, p. 253.

Ranyard R, Hebenton B. and Pease K, (1994), "An Analysis of a Guideline Case as Applied to the Offence of Rape", *Howard Journal of Criminal Justice*, Vol. 33, No. 3, p. 203.

Radzinowicz L. (1966), *Ideology and Crime*, Heinemann, London.

Report of the Roskill Committee on Fraud Trials (1986), HMSO, London.

Robertshaw P. (1994), "Sentencing Rapists: First Tier Courts in 1991-92" , *Criminal Law Review*, p. 343.

Royal Commission on Criminal Justice (1993), Report (Chairman Viscount Runciman of Doxford), Cmn. 2263, HMSO, London.

Sallon C. and Bedingfield D. (1993), "Drugs, Money and the Law", *Criminal Law Review*, p. 165.

Scottish Council on Crime (1975), *Crime and the Prevention of Crime*, HMSO, Edinburgh.

Shoham S. (1969), "Sentencing Policy of Criminal Courts in Israel", *Journal of Criminal Law, Criminology and Police Science*, Vol. 50, p. 327.

Shulhofer S. and Nagel I. (1990), "Negotiated Pleas under the Federal Sentencing Guidelines: The First Fifteen Months", *American Criminal Law Review*, p. 231.

Shute S, (1994), "Prosecution Appeals Against Sentence: The First Five Years", *Modern Law Review*, Vol. 57, p. 745.

Smith A.B. and Blumberg A.S. (1967), "The Problem of Objectivity in Judicial Decision-Making", *Social Forces*, Vol. 46, p. 96.

Smith A.T.H. (1992), "Legislating the Criminal Code: The Law Commission's Proposals", *Criminal Law Review*, p. 396.

Smith J.C. and Hogan B. (1992), *Criminal Law*, Butterworths, London.

Solivetti L.M. (1994), "Drug Diffusion and Social Change: The Illusion about a Formal Social Control", *Howard Journal of Criminal Justice*, Vol. 33, No. 1, p. 41.

Spencer J.N. (1991), "Judicial Review of Criminal Proceedings", *Criminal Law Review*, p. 259.

Steadman H. and Cocozza, J. (1974), *Careers of the Criminally Insane*, Heath and Co., Lexington D.C.

Stone J. (1945), *The Province and Function of Law*, Associated General Publications, Sydney.

Stone J. (1966), *Social Dimensions of Law and Justice*, Stevens and Sons, London.

Stone J. (1979), "Justice not equality", in Kamenka E. and Tay A.E-S. (eds), *Justice*, Edward Arnold, London.

Szasz T.S. (1960), "The Myth of Mental Illness", *American Psychologist*, Vol. 15, p. 113.

Tarling R. (1979), *Sentencing Practice in Magistrates' Courts*, Home Office Research Unit Study No. 56, HMSO, London.

Thomas D.A. (1967), "Sentencing - The Basic Principles", *Criminal Law Review*, p. 453.

Thomas D.A. (1970), (1979), *Principles of Sentencing*, 1st and 2nd editions, Heinemann, London.

Thomas D.A. (1982), Commentary on *R v Routley*, *Criminal Law Review*, p. 383.

Thomas D.A. (1983), Commentary on *R v de Havilland*, *Criminal Law Review*, p. 491.

Thomas D.A. (1989), "The Criminal Justice Act: (4) The Sentencing Provisions", *Criminal Law Review*, p. 53.

Thomas D.A. (1992a), "Towards a new tariff", *Sentencing News*, No. 4, p. 12.

Thomas D.A. (1992b), "The Criminal Justice Act 1991 (1) Custodial Sentences", *Criminal Law Review*, p. 232.

Thomas D.A. (1993a), "Statutory aggravation", *Sentencing News*, No. 5, p. 12.

Thomas D.A. (1993b), Commentary on *R v Cunningham*, *Criminal Law Review*, p. 149 and Case Notes 143-157.

Thomas D.A. (1993c), Commentary on *R v Coull*, *Criminal Law Review*, p. 978.

Thomas D.A. (1993d), Viewpoint, *Sentencing News*, No. 3, p. 12.

Thomas D.A. (1993e), Commentary on *Attorney-General's Reference (No. 4 of 1993) (R v Bingham)*, *Criminal Law Review*, p. 705.

Thomas D.A. (1993f), Commentary on *R v Cameron, R v Huntley*, *Criminal Law Review*, p. 722.

Thomas D.A. (1993g), Comment, *Sentencing News*, No. 2, p.11.

Thomas D.A. (1994a), "Larger than normal sentences", *Sentencing News*, No. 2, p.7

Thomas D.A. (1994b), Viewpoint, *Sentencing News*, No. 2. p.12.

Thomas D.A. (1994c), Citing sentencing decisions, *Sentencing News*, No. 3. p.7.

Thomas D.A. (1994d), Commentary on *R v Bradley*, *Criminal Law Review*, p. 382.

Thomas D.A. (1995), Commentary on *R v Townsend*, *Criminal Law Review*, p. 182.

Thomas D.A. *Current Sentencing Practice*, Sweet and Maxwell, London.

Tonry M. and Coffee J.C. (1992), "Plea Bargaining and Enforcement of Sentencing Guidelines", in von Hirsch A. and Ashworth A. (eds), *Principled Sentencing*, Edinburgh University Press, Edinburgh.

Uotila J. (ed.) (1985), *The Finnish Legal System*, Finnish Lawyers Publishing Co., Helsinki.

Von Hirsch A. (1976), *Doing Justice: The Choice of Punishments*, Hill and Wang, New York.

Von Hirsch A. (1986), *Past or Future Crimes*, Manchester University Press, Manchester.

Von Hirsch A. (1986), "Deservedness and Dangerousness in Sentencing Policy", *Criminal Law Review*, p. 79.

Von Hirsch A. (1987), "Guidance by numbers or words? Numerical versus narrative guidelines for sentencing", in Pease K. and Wasik M. (eds), *Sentencing Reform*, Manchester University Press, Manchester.

Von Hirsch A. (1992), "Ordinal and Cardinal Desert", in von Hirsch A. and Ashworth A.J. (eds), *Principled Sentencing*, Edinburgh University Press, Edinburgh.

Von Hirsch A. and Jareborg N. (1989), "Sweden's Sentencing Statute Enacted", *Criminal Law Review*, p. 275.

Walker N. (1980), *Punishment, Danger and Stigma*, Basil Blackwell, Oxford.

Walker N. (1982), "Unscientific, Unwise, Unprofitable or Unjust?", *British Journal of Criminology*, Vol. 22, p. 276.

Walker N. (1985), *Sentencing Theory, Law and Practice*, Butterworths, London.

Walker N. and Hough M. (eds), (1988), *Public Attitudes to Sentencing: Surveys in Five Counties*, Gower, Aldershot.

Wasik M. (1981), "Sentencing Disparity and the Role of the Court of Appeal", *Justice of the Peace*, Vol. 145, p. 348.

Wasik M. (1984), "Sentencing and the Divisional Court", *Criminal Law*

Review, p. 272.

Wasik M. (1993), *Emmins on Sentencing*, 2nd ed., Blackstone Press, London.

Wasik M. and Taylor R.D. (1994), *Blackstone's Guide to the Criminal Justice Act 1991*, Blackstone Press, London.

Wasik M. and Taylor R. (1995), *Blackstone's Guide to the Criminal Justice and Public Order Act 1994*, Blackstone Press, London.

Wasik M. and von Hirsch A. (1990), "Statutory Sentencing Principle: The 1990 White Paper", *Modern Law Review*, Vol. 53, p. 508.

Wasik M. and Turner A. (1993), "Sentencing Guidelines for Magistrates' Courts", *Criminal Law Review*, p. 345.

Wasik M. and von Hirsch A. (1994), "Section 29 Revised: Previous Convictions in Sentencing", *Criminal Law Review*, p. 409.

Wells C. (1986), "Codification of the Criminal Law (4) Restatement or Reform", *Criminal Law Review*, p. 314.

Wenk E., Robinson J. and Smith G. (1972), "Can Violence be Predicted?" *Crime and Delinquency*, Vol. 18, p. 393.

Wheeler S. (ed.), (1968), *Controlling Delinquents*, John Wiley, New York.

Whynes D.K. and Bean P. (eds), (1991), *Policing and Prescribing*, Macmillan, Basingstoke.

Williams G. (1983), *Textbook of Criminal Law*, Stevens and Sons, London.

Williams G. (1990), "Force, injury and serious injury", *New Law Journal*, p. 1227.

Wood D. (1988), "Dangerous Offenders, and the Morality of Protective Sentencing", *Criminal Law Review*, p. 424.

Woolf, Sir H. (1991), *Prison Disturbances, April 1990, Report of an Inquiry*, HMSO, London.

Wooton B. (1981), *Crime and the Criminal Law*, 2nd edition, Stevens, London.

Zander M. (1986), "The Report of the Roskill Committee on Fraud Trials", *Criminal Law Review*, p. 423.